SOCIAL & CULTURAL ANTHROPOLOGY

SOCIAL & CULTURAL ANTHROPOLOGY

•

John Monaghan and Peter Just

A BRIEF
INSIGHT

STERLING

New York / London
www.sterlingpublishing.com

STERLING and the distinctive Sterling logo are registered trademarks of
Sterling Publishing Co., Inc.

Library of Congress Cataloging-in-Publication Data Available

10 9 8 7 6 5 4 3 2 1

Published by Sterling Publishing Co., Inc.
387 Park Avenue South, New York, NY 10016

Published by arrangement with Oxford University Press, Inc.

© 2000 by John Monaghan and Peter Just
Illustrated edition published in 2010 by Sterling Publishing Co., Inc.
Additional text © 2010 Sterling Publishing Co., Inc.

Distributed in Canada by Sterling Publishing
c/o Canadian Manda Group, 165 Dufferin Street
Toronto, Ontario, Canada M6K 3H6

Book design: The DesignWorks Group

Please see picture credits on page 215 for image copyright information.

Printed in China
All rights reserved

Sterling ISBN 978-1-4027-6881-1

For information about custom editions, special sales, premium and
corporate purchases, please contact Sterling Special Sales Department at
800-805-5489 or specialsales@sterlingpublishing.com.

Frontispiece: These women are dressed in the beautiful *huipiles*, or
blouses, characteristic of indigenous people of Mesoamerica. Nearly every
town has its own *huipil* style, color scheme, and decorative pattern. This
group is from the state of Oaxaca, Mexico.

CONTENTS

•

To our children

Lee Ann, Lizzy, Emmy, and Ben

•

INTRODUCTION

●

FOR OVER TWENTY YEARS we have been talking about what anthropology is, how to do it, and how best to communicate what we know. This dialogue began when we were graduate students at the University of Pennsylvania, learning to be anthropologists. We continued to exchange ideas after we went off to do fieldwork—an exercise at the core of our discipline and something we will have a lot to say about in the first chapter. But what enhanced our conversation more than anything was our experience of becoming teachers. The task of introducing anthropology to thousands of educated nonspecialists over the years has convinced us that the best way to do this is to emphasize not so much what anthropologists have discovered, but how anthropologists think about what they have learned—concepts over facts if you will. This means we will not be as

Dou Donggo women in Doro Ntika preparing rice for cooking. One is pounding to separate husk from grain, another is winnowing, and others stand by watching.

concerned with reviewing the latest trends as with trying to look at the issues that have been at the heart of anthropological inquiry and with trying to convey what has been of enduring value in our discipline.

Anthropology grew out of the intersection of European discovery, colonialism, and natural science. In the nineteenth century the first anthropologists, influenced by the same philosophical currents that led to the Darwinian revolution, were interested in reconstructing stages of social and cultural evolution. Figures such as Edward Tylor and Lewis Henry Morgan published influential works tracing everything from writing systems to marriage practices from their most

Englishman Sir Edward Burnett Tylor (1832–1917) and American Lewis Henry Morgan (1818–81), both shown here in undated portraits, studied the cultures of Mexicans and Native Americans, respectively, and contributed valuable information to the emerging fields of modern ethnology and anthropology.

primitive origins to their modern manifestations. By the beginning of the last century anthropologists had developed other intellectual projects and, most importantly, were no longer content to rely on the accounts of colonial officials, missionaries, travelers, and other nonspecialists for their primary data. They began to go into the "field" as ethnographers to gather their own information firsthand. Although anthropology has changed quite a bit since the time of these ethnographic pioneers, ethnography remains one of the things that distinguish anthropology from the rest of the social sciences, and the importance of doing ethnography is perhaps the one thing that all anthropologists agree upon.

In the early part of the twentieth century anthropology was typically concerned with small-scale, technologically simple societies. In part this was out of a desire to record ways of life that were rapidly changing with the advent of colonialism (although it would be a mistake to assume that these societies were somehow unchanging, or even truly isolated, before their contact with the West) and in part it was out of a desire to get at the "essential" or "elementary" forms of human institutions (although it would also be a mistake to assume that matters such as law or religion are somehow more "basic" in these societies). In the latter part of the twentieth century mainstream anthropology has moved away from a vision of itself as a science in the tradition of the physical sciences and has adopted a more interpretative, humanistic approach. It has also shifted its focus from an exclusive concern with non-Western, small-scale rural societies to groups that would have been the purview of sociology, such as labor unions, social clubs, and migrant communities found in urban and industrialized settings. Nonetheless, anthropology remains broadly comparative in its scope, taking *all* societies into account and treating them all as equally significant. At the same time anthropology continues to be firmly rooted in the descriptive richness that comes out of the specific encounters anthropologists have with particular peoples and places. Often we have found our greatest strengths to be those of the storyteller. Throughout this book we will be illustrating our presentation with anecdotes from our fieldwork. This, by the way, is quite typical for anthropologists, for whom the immediacy of the encounter with an exotic culture never really fades. So let us tell you a bit about the two societies with which we are the most familiar.

Peter did his primary research among the Dou Donggo for two years in the early 1980s, with several subsequent shorter visits. At the time the Dou Donggo numbered around twenty thousand people, living in the highland massif that sweeps up on the west side of Bima Bay, a spectacular natural harbor in the eastern end of the island of Sumbawa. Sumbawa lies about midway in the long arc of islands stretching from Sumatra to Timor in Indonesia; it is the second major island east of Bali. The eastern half of Sumbawa is called Bima (although that is not the local name) and is mostly occupied by a much larger ethnic group who call themselves Dou Mbojo and are usually referred to as the Bimanese by outsiders. As part of the ancient Javanese Majapahit Empire, Bima was a Hindu kingdom. When that empire collapsed in the early seventeenth century, Bima and her people became Muslim and today are known as among the most fervent Muslims in Indonesia (a country where perhaps 85 percent of the population confess that faith). The Dou Donggo, however, had remained outside the Bimanese kingdom while it was a Hindu

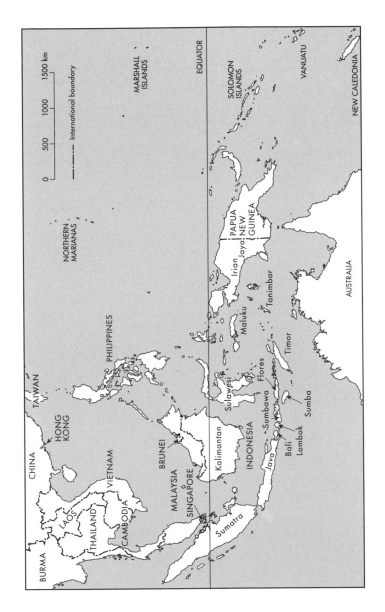

Indonesia

Although much of Bima, the eastern half of the island of Sumbawa, Indonesia, was a Hindu kingdom and a part of the ancient Javanese Majapahit Empire, when the Hindu kingdom collapsed, Bima became Muslim. Its people are now known as some of the most fervent Muslims in Indonesia. This limestone figure of a Brahminic ascetic is from the late Majapahit Empire.

kingdom, and became part of the Muslim Sultanate of Bima only much later and by treaty rather than by conquest. They were able to retain their relative independence in part because they had a reputation as fierce warriors and in part because their mountainous territory was relatively easy to defend (Dou Donggo means "Mountain People"). Although they became part of Muslim Bima, the Dou Donggo retained certain political privileges and did not, by and large, accept Islam, but held fast to their indigenous religious beliefs and practices. It was their stalwart refusal to accept the religion of their suzerain and neighbors that first interested Peter in the Dou Donggo. He set out to see what role this might have played in establishing an ethnic boundary between the Dou Donggo and the Bimanese, despite the fact that they share a common language (Nggahi Mbojo). By the time of Peter's first survey trip to Donggo (as the district is most sensibly called) most Dou

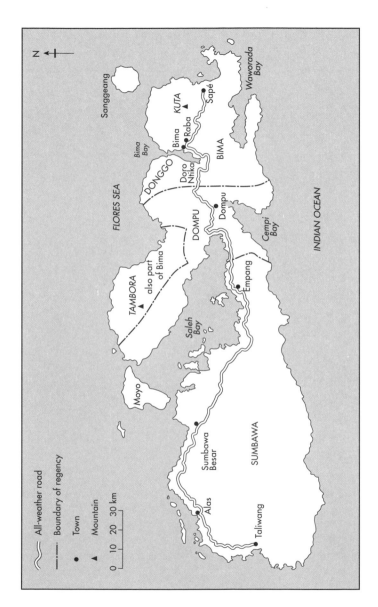

Sumbawa

Donggo had accepted either Islam or Christianity, although as the local Roman Catholic catechist put it, "The people are 70 percent Muslim, 30 percent Catholic, and 90 percent *kaffir* [pagan]." Studying religious beliefs became a major focus of Peter's fieldwork as did studying the way the people went about resolving disputes.

When Peter returned to Donggo in 1981 for a two-year stay, he was accompanied by his wife, Anne, who was, to put it mildly, a real trouper. They lived in the village of Doro Ntika, the oldest and, with a population of about three thousand spread over several hamlets, the largest of Donggo's traditional villages. Conditions were quite primitive: Doro Ntika had no running water, no electricity, no paved roads. The houses, on the other hand, were comfortable, built of teak and resting on stilts five feet (one and a half meters) high or more, with roofs of thatch, tile, or galvanized iron. The local economy was in something of a transitional period. Formerly the people had had a relatively self-sufficient subsistence by means of the cultivation of swidden rice, maize, and millet, supplemented with bananas, coconuts, and other fruits together with products gathered from the mountain forest (including the most wonderful honey!). Swidden agriculture depends on burning tracts of forest, cultivating the land for a year or two, and then allowing the forest to regenerate. Increasing population densities, however, had put too much stress on the land to allow for complete forest regeneration, and much of the land was taken over by growths of weedy shrubs, much reducing its fertility. Increasingly the people of Doro Ntika were shifting to the cultivation of wet rice in terraced paddy fields and the cultivation of cash crops such as peanuts and soybeans for sale in lowland markets. Although the population was growing rapidly because of the introduction of modern medicine, diseases such as malaria, tuberculosis, and dysentery still took a heavy toll, especially among the infants and children of the village.

Despite the difficulties of life in these circumstances Peter and Anne found the Dou Donggo to be warm, generous, and ever ready to tease and joke. With the help of a rather roguish village headman, Peter and Anne were able to borrow a house which they furnished with goods available in Bima Town—including a kerosene stove that created a minor sensation, as everyone else in the village cooked over wood fires. Doro Ntika is built on a high ridge between river gorges; the houses are built on terraces cut into the steep sides of the ridge. In time Peter and Anne acquired two ponies which they used for transportation and to carry water up from the river. From time to time they would go down to Bima Town to collect their mail and replenish food supplies not available in Donggo. While there they stayed with the family of Haji M. Djafar Amyn, who were exceptionally generous hosts, so Peter and Anne were able to get an intimate look at life also among the lowland Bimanese. With the exception of several vacations to Bali and other parts of Indonesia, Peter and Anne lived there for two years. It was an unforgettable experience.

John did his primary field research among the Mixtec of Santiago Nuyoo in the southern Mexican state of Oaxaca. His longest period of fieldwork lasted from 1983 to 1986, but he has returned almost every year since. Mixtec speakers, who number just over four hundred thousand, are the third largest indigenous group in Mexico. In the sixteenth century the Mixtec were divided into dozens of small kingdoms whose ruling élite patronized one of the finest artistic traditions in the New World. We know a great deal about preconquest Mixtec life from the large corpus of Mixtec books that survived and because Mixtec scribes continued to produce works using the native script for almost eighty years after the Spanish took over. After their conquest by the Spanish, the Mixtec suffered a catastrophic demographic collapse, as millions of people throughout the Americas succumbed to Old World diseases and the abuse they

Because Mixtec scribes continued to use their native script for almost eighty years after the Spanish conquest, much information is still available about preconquest Mixtec life and experiences under early colonial rule. This fragment from the Codex Vindobonensis, a book painted before the Spanish arrived in the Americas, shows Dzahui, the holy rain.

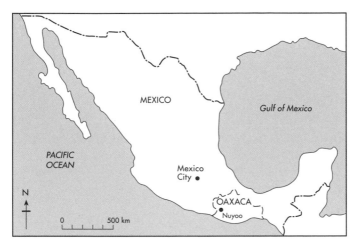

Mexico showing Oaxaca region

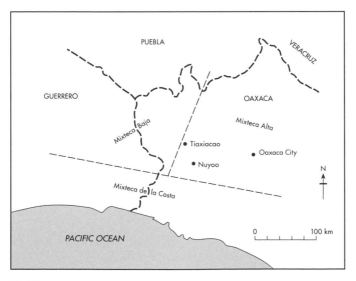

The Mixteca

suffered at the hands of colonialists. Although the Mixtec population has grown since the end of the sixteenth century, it is still not the size it was before the arrival of the Spanish.

The Mixteca, the homeland Mixtec speakers share with several other indigenous groups as well as communities of mestizos and Afro-Mexicans, is ecologically diverse, having a broad coastal savannah, tropical forests, high, pine-forested mountains, fertile riverbeds, and arid deserts. The Mixtec live scattered across the landscape in small towns and villages. Santiago Nuyoo, the village where John has done most of his fieldwork, has a population of about three thousand people, with about a quarter of its inhabitants living in the town center and the rest distributed among five hamlets. Nuyoo and its neighbor Santa María Yucuhiti sit at the head of a narrow canyon, with beautiful waterfalls flowing down the canyon sides. The landscape is extremely rocky and there are almost no level plots (Nuyootecos will often say good-bye to one another by calling out "don't fall"). But owing to its relatively low elevation and abundant rainfall the area is known as the "garden of the Mixteca." Oranges, mangoes, and *zapote* grow wild, rare orchids cling to the trees, and a pine forest covers the surrounding mountains. Nuyootecos specialize in the cultivation of maize, almost all of it grown through swidden techniques; they also grow cash crops, principally bananas and coffee. Although wage migration has been a fact of life for the Mixtec for hundreds of years, since the 1950s increasing numbers of Nuyootecos have left the Mixteca: at first they traveled to Veracruz and Morelos to find work harvesting coffee and other crops; then in the 1960s they began to travel to Mexico City, where they worked in bakeries, factories, and the service economy; and finally in the late 1980s, a few men made their way to the United States, where they worked on a ranch in Texas. John's research focused on how Nuyootecos maintain a strong sense of community in the face of these changes and dislocations.

Although John's wife, the archaeologist Laura Junker, did not live with him during his initial period of fieldwork (she was pursuing her Ph.D. in anthropology), she did spend several months in Nuyoo. Later, after their children were born, the whole family came to the Mixteca to visit. Like the Dou Donggo, the Mixtec enjoy a good joke, and despite the numerous photographic essays of indigenous Mexican people that portray everyone with grim, determined, or overwhelmed looks on their faces, when they are among themselves Nuyootecos turn out to be great pranksters and masters of understatement. John realized he had finally got the measure of them after meeting a group of men on a path outside town. They asked him what kind of food he and his wife were going to serve at an upcoming fiesta they were hosting. John and Laura were able to afford to serve choice cuts of meat, but they were, at the same time, outsiders with strange tastes. John managed to deliver his reply, "we are going to slaughter a couple of thin and mangy dogs," with so little change of expression that the men all paused before going off hooting with laughter. John owes much of what he knows about the Mixtec to the Pérez Sarabia, Pérez Pérez, and Modesto Velasco families, who took him in, allowed him to live with them, and by asking him to be the godfather of one of their children, made him a relative.

No short introduction could hope to do justice to the breadth and complexity of contemporary anthropological studies. At the end of the twentieth century the Royal Anthropological Institute had over twenty-three hundred members; the American Anthropological Association had over eleven thousand members. France, too, was the home of a rich and deeply influential school of anthropology. Most exciting, perhaps, has been the growth of anthropology in Latin America and in former European colonies, prominently India and New Guinea. Each of these nations, along with industrial nations such as Australia and Japan, has begun to develop its own intellectual traditions and research agendas. Obviously we could not provide you with a survey of anthropology that would begin to cover all the perspectives and projects these anthropologists engage. Instead we have tried to focus our introduction on those "big" questions that have occupied the attentions of anthropologists since the beginnings of the discipline: what is unique about human beings? how are groups of people—family, class, tribe, nation—formed and what holds them together? what is the nature of belief, economic exchange, the self? how are we to go about researching and understanding such things? And rather than try to provide you with a sense of what the "cutting edge" of anthropological theory is today—a picture sure to become obsolete as soon as it is published—we have chosen to acquaint you with the ideas at the roots of the discipline, and with the thinkers whom all anthropologists share as intellectual forebears.

In the first chapter we introduce you to anthropology by trying to give you an idea of what it is that anthropologists do. In the next two chapters we look at culture (traditionally an American preoccupation) and society (traditionally a British one), the twin conceptual towers on which anthropology is founded. In the next two chapters we look at the most basic ways in which human beings form social ties, first through ties of blood and marriage, and then through larger social groups such as tribe, ethnic group, and nation. In the final three chapters we look briefly at issues of economy, religion, and identity, topics that have attracted anthropologists for generations, and in which, we feel, some of the most interesting classic work has been done. We have necessarily left out many fascinating subdisciplines: medical anthropology, the anthropology of law, the anthropology of science and technology, to name but a few. Any of these could easily be the topic of its own introduction and in this regard we can only urge you to take this book as the narrow opening of a very wide door and hope that it will inspire you to explore much further.

ONE

A Dispute in Donggo: Fieldwork and Ethnography

•

AS HAS OFTEN BEEN SAID, IF YOU want to understand what anthropology *is*, look at what anthropologists *do*. Above all else, what anthropologists do is *ethnography*. Ethnography is to the cultural or social anthropologist what lab research is to the biologist, what archival research is to the historian, or what survey research is to the sociologist. Often called— not altogether accurately—"participant observation," ethnography is based on the apparently simple idea that in order to understand what people are up to, it is best to observe them by interacting with them intimately and over an extended period. That is why anthropologists have tended traditionally to spend long periods—sometimes years at a stretch—living in the communities they study, sharing the lives of the people to as great an extent as they can. It is this approach that has defined our discipline and distinguished it from other social sciences. Now, we certainly do not

Nineteenth-century Indonesian shadow puppets representing the sage Begawan Bisma and a maidservant.

dismiss the methods more characteristic of other disciplines, such as the use of questionnaires or the collection of quantitative behavioral data. But anthropologists have long felt that approaching the study of human beings in those ways is likely to produce an incomplete—even misleading— understanding of the people studied, especially when those people are members of foreign or unfamiliar societies.

It might also be said that fieldwork is what gives the enterprise of anthropology a good deal of its romance. It was certainly one of the things that attracted the two of us to the discipline. Today anthropologists conduct fieldwork in settings that are as unexotic as television stations in city centers, magistrates' courts in small towns, corporate boardrooms, and church congregations in middle-class suburbs. But in its infancy as a profession, anthropology was distinguished by its concentration on so-called primitive societies: relatively small, non-Western communities in which social institutions appeared to be fairly limited and simple (not so, as it turned out!) and social interaction was conducted almost entirely face-to-face. Such societies, it was felt, provided anthropologists with a simplified view of the "elementary" workings of society, one that contrasted with the complexities of "modern" (that is, Western) society. There was also a sense among anthropologists that the ways of life represented by these smaller societies were rapidly disappearing, and since many of them had no writing, it was an urgent task to preserve a record for posterity. This orientation of the discipline, and an early commitment to the firsthand collection of ethnographic data by means of participant observation, led anthropologists to some of the most remote and exotic places on earth. Most often working alone and in isolation from other Westerners, the ethnographer cut a bold figure indeed. Often this isolation created a sense of alienation and loneliness, especially in the early stages of fieldwork. But almost all anthropologists find themselves assimilating to the culture of their host communities to a greater or lesser degree—a few, it is said, even to the point of "going native," completely adopting the lifestyle of their hosts and never returning home. Altogether, the process of immersing oneself in fieldwork can be a challenging and unique experience, one that continues to attract men and women to anthropology. It also so happens that participant observation seems to be the most effective way of understanding in depth the ways in which other people see the world and interact with it, and often provides a check on our own preconceptions and beliefs.

Let us begin with a story, a story that shows you not only how anthropologists work, but what is distinctive about anthropology as a discipline. This is a story about Peter's fieldwork with the Dou Donggo and how he came to be interested in the anthropology of law.

One night I was sitting in the house of a friend in Doro Ntika, the village where I was conducting fieldwork. One of my friend's relatives burst into the room, shouting that his sister-in-law, a woman named ina Mone, had been assaulted by a young man, la Ninde. We rushed over to ina Mone's house to see what had happened. Ina Mone sat on the floor of the room, one side of her face painted with a medicinal paste, where she said la Ninde had struck her. She also showed us the shirt she had been wearing and that had been torn in the assault. Her male relatives were angry, and talked of "taking down the spears and sharpening the bushknives," anxious to exact an immediate revenge on la Ninde. But everyone became calmer when ama Tife, one of the principal elders of the village, came by to assure us that he and the other elders of Doro Ntika would convene a court and exact justice according to tradition. The next morning they did just that. La Ninde was brought before a group of elders with most of the village looking on. Ina Mone showed her medicated face and torn shirt as evidence. La Ninde admitted to having shouted at her, but denied having laid hands upon her. A spirited and tumultuous drama ensued, as members of the court, led by ama Panci, berated la Ninde and finally extracted a confession. He was assessed a minor fine and was made to kneel before ina Mone begging forgiveness. She gave him a symbolic slap on the head, and he was let go.

Later that afternoon, I chatted with a friend. I said, "Wasn't that terrible, what la Ninde did, assaulting ina Mone like that?" He answered, "Yes, it was. But you know he never really hit her." I was surprised. "What about the torn shirt and her face?" I asked. "Well," he said, "anyone can

Ama Tife. Ama Tife was the elder who assured ina Mone's kin that they would receive justice from a panel of village elders. In addition to his talents as a judge, ama Tife was a skilled healer and ritual specialist.

tear a shirt, and who knows what's under the medicine." I was deeply shocked. "But that means la Ninde is innocent. Isn't this terribly unfair?" "Not at all," he replied. "What la Ninde was convicted of was more true than what really happened." He then proceeded to fill me in on what everyone else in the village knew, indeed, what they had known all along. Ina Mone had seen la Ninde hanging around la Fia, a young woman who was betrothed to another young man, absent from Doro Ntika. Ina Mone had complained to la Ninde's mother, who in turn had admonished la Ninde. Furious at having been ratted out, la Ninde had gone to ina Mone's house and threatened her—a serious breach of etiquette—but had not in fact assaulted her.

This story is an account of a real event in the real world, as witnessed by an ethnographer. How would this event have been recorded and analyzed by a historian or a sociologist? To begin with, to a historian who works primarily with archives or court records, the case of la Ninde's assault on ina Mone would be completely invisible. The Dou Donggo do not keep written records of disputes settled by village elders, so this case and the great majority of cases would not appear in a form accessible to the historian working in an archive. Even a historian who adopts the ethnographic methods of an anthropologist and takes down oral histories might have difficulty in accessing this case, for among the Dou Donggo it is an accepted practice that one never discusses a dispute after it has been settled. Only because he was on the scene at the time the dispute erupted was Peter able to record it and explore its meaning.

How would this case have appeared to a sociologist or a criminologist? Although some sociologists and criminologists are adept at using ethnographic methods, it is far more common for them to rely on surveys, questionnaires, and the analysis of official statistics. Again, to those relying on official statistics, this case would have been completely invisible. La Ninde's "assault" might have appeared as a "data point" in a survey of disputes in the community undertaken by a sociologist. But it seems unlikely that a survey would be so artfully constructed as to see beyond the superficial evidence of the case, or, more importantly, to uncover the notion that la Ninde's conviction of a crime he did not commit was "more true than what really happened." If the case *had* been recorded officially, researchers (including anthropologists) who rely on such data would probably assume the case of la Ninde was one of simple assault, leading to conclusions about Dou Donggo society that would be seriously incomplete, if not misleading.

Very well, then, what might the case described mean to an ethnographer? How might an anthropologist analyze this event to learn more about what the Dou Donggo believe and how they behave? First, after considerable questioning, it became clear to Peter that the case had little to do with assault and a very great deal to do with respect for the institution of marriage. Why had ina Mone complained to la Ninde's mother about his flirtations with la Fia? Because ina Mone had a real and vested interest in protecting the integrity of betrothals, particularly betrothals contracted by the family of ama Panci. Why? Because ina Mone's daughter was betrothed to ama Panci's son and another of ama Panci's sons was betrothed to la Fia!

One lesson, then, that Peter learned was that in disputes (at least among the Dou Donggo) things are often other than what they appear to be. A case of "assault" may really be a case about "alienation of affection." What made this sort of realization possible? First of all, Peter was there to witness the event to begin with, something that would not have been possible had he not spent almost two years in this village. The ability to observe unusual, unique events is one of the principal advantages of the

A Dou Donggo judge. This is ama Balo, another prominent Dou Donggo elder, as he is engaged in settling a dispute. Dou Donggo dispute settlement, like law in many small-scale societies, stresses consensus and the restoration of ruptured social relationships rather than a winner-take-all decision of guilt or innocence.

ethnographic method. It is important to recognize, as well, that Peter was able to observe the case in question from the outset not only because he lived in Doro Ntika for a long time, but because he lived there around the clock and as a member of the community. The case came to his attention not because he was seeking out information on disputes or even on betrothals, but because he just happened to be chatting with friends in a nearby house, long after a conventional "working day" was over. It is this openness to the serendipitous discovery that gives the ethnographic method strength and flexibility not generally available to highly deductive social science methods, such as survey or statistical research. Indeed, anthropologists often find themselves doing significant research on unanticipated subjects. While there are those research topics we take with us to the field, there are also topics imposed upon us by the actual circumstances and events of people's everyday lives. Peter had not intended to study dispute settlement when he set off for Indonesia, but neither could he ignore the research opportunity he encountered that evening. The randomness of ethnographic serendipity is compensated for by the length of time a good ethnographer spends in the field; eventually, one hopes, one will accidentally encounter most social phenomena of significance.

Prolonged exposure to daily life in Doro Ntika also made Peter aware that it was necessary to look beyond the superficial events of the case, made him aware that issues like the fidelity of fiancés was a sensitive, even explosive, topic in this community. In other words, after more than a year living in this community, Peter had a rich and nuanced context into which the events of this case could be placed. The discrepancy between what a social event is apparently about and what it might "really" be about is almost impossible to discern without the experiential context ethnographic fieldwork makes available. That is one of the advantages that anthropologists have traditionally relied upon for the insights they derive from their research and it is why traditional ethnographic fieldwork has placed a premium on long duration—often as much as two years for an initial study. Moreover, Peter was able to discover what the case was "really about" because his long residence in the village had allowed him to build up relations of trust with people who were willing to confide in him and to explain events and motivations beyond superficial appearances. Having long-term cordial relations with people in the village—having friends, if you like—also enabled Peter to persist in his questions beyond the superficial and to evaluate the content of the answers he received.

What implications might an anthropologist see in the lessons of this case? Every ethnographic description at least implicitly participates in the cross-cultural comparisons that also engage anthropologists. Anthropology has long been engaged in relating the description of local beliefs and practices to categories of universal, pan-human significance. The case of la Ninde compelled Peter to bring into question his understanding of legal categories like "evidence" and "liability," to question the universality of the idea of "justice" itself. What does it mean that virtually everyone in the village knew the physical evidence presented by ina Mone was false, yet was nonetheless accepted? What might it mean for our understanding of liability and responsibility if la Ninde could be convicted for what he *might have done*, rather than for what he actually did, without producing a sense among the villagers that he was a victim of trumpery or injustice? If evidence and liability could be handled in this way, what does that mean if we are to try to construct a sense of what justice means to human beings at large? It is this interplay between the specific and the general, between the local and the universal, that gives anthropology much of its value as a social science. For not only are we engaged in recording the "customs and manners" of people around the world; we are constantly bringing our appreciation of local knowledge to bear on a more general understanding of what it means to be a human being. We will have more to say about this process in the next chapter.

Fieldwork: Strategies and Practices

It should be obvious that a truly comprehensive description of any society's culture is far beyond the capacity of even a hundred researchers. An ethnographer goes to the field with the intention of studying some particular aspect of social life, which might range from ecological adaptation to indigenous theology, to relations between the genders, to grassroots political mobilization, and so on (see sidebar on page 29). The ethnographer does not enter into the enterprise unprepared. What ethnographers need to know is as diverse and varied as the studies they undertake. Most anthropologists begin their preparation with several years of study in the history and previous ethnographic literature of the region in which they propose to do fieldwork. Because anthropologists have felt it imperative that they conduct their fieldwork in the language of the people they study without using translators, an ethnographer may need to acquire at least passable fluency in several languages. In addition to such general preparation, ethnographers are usually trained in more specialized fields concerning the kind of problem they intend to investigate. A researcher who intends to study the medicinal use of plants among an Amazonian people, for example, not only needs to learn a good deal of conventional botany, but also needs to be familiar with how various of the world's peoples have categorized and used plants. Anthropologists are always anthropologists *of* something and somewhere: John is an anthropologist of religion and a Mesoamericanist; Peter is an anthropologist of law and a Southeast Asianist.

An ethnographer's first task is to become established in the community. This is often a protracted and difficult process, during which more than a few projects have foundered. Once the ethnographer has found a source of funding for the project, it is often necessary to secure a variety

Participant observation allows anthropologists to relate the description of local beliefs and practices to categories of universal, pan-human significance. This photograph taken in 1953 shows anthropologist Margaret Mead conversing with a Manus mother and child during fieldwork on the Admiralty Islands (now part of Papua New Guinea).

of permits from various levels of government, local research institutions, and the host community. This can consume more than a year of the ethnographer's time, before he or she even sets foot in the field site. One colleague carrying out a research project at the headquarters of a major industrial concern needed to have his proposal reviewed by the company's lawyers before he could even enter the building to talk with anyone. Once they have arrived, ethnographers face many of the same problems anyone would encounter when moving into a new community, problems complicated by unfamiliarity with the language and the challenges of daily life in places lacking many of the amenities they may have been used to at home: electricity, indoor plumbing, or easy access to health care, news, or entertainment. Many anthropologists work in cities and suburbs in Europe and North America, where the challenges are of a different nature. Neither of us would be eager to trade places with colleagues we know who have worked with drug addicts in Spanish Harlem or the top executives of a multinational corporation in Philadelphia.

The ethnographer faces more subtle difficulties, too. Locally powerful individuals may try to use the ethnographer as a prize or a pawn in their rivalries. Members of the community may have an exaggerated idea of what the ethnographer can do for them, and make persistent demands that cannot be met. At the same time, the ethnographer often experiences the great joy of making new friends and the thrill of seeing and doing things he or she would never otherwise have been able to see or do. As a day-to-day experience, fieldwork can be filled with abruptly alternating emotional highs and lows. At its heart the process of doing ethnography really is participant observation. By living among the people of the community as they themselves live, the ethnographer stands the best chance of becoming established.

· · · · ·

HALF A DOZEN ETHNOGRAPHIES

To give an idea of the range of people and places anthropologists study, here, in no particular order, are the titles of half a dozen ethnographies, each with a very brief description.

We Eat the Mines and the Mines Eat Us: June Nash's description of Bolivian tin miners and the ways in which transnational economic processes affect their lives (1979).

Beamtimes and Lifetimes: Sharon Traweek's account of the world of high-energy physicists (1988).

Tuhami: Portrait of a Moroccan: Vincent Crapanzano's ethnographic biography describes his encounter with "an illiterate Moroccan tilemaker who believes himself married to a camel-footed she-demon" (1980).

In the Realm of the Diamond Queen: Anna Tsing's study of political and cultural marginality, linking a Borneo people to the Indonesian nation and the global politics of "modernization" (1993).

The Channeling Zone: American Spirituality in an Anxious Age: Michael F. Brown presents a fascinating look at the lives and experiences of New Age "channelers" and their place in contemporary American spiritual life (1997).

Medusa's Hair: Gananath Obeyesekere brings insights from psychoanalysis to bear on "personal symbols and religious experience" among ecstatic priests and priestesses in Sri Lanka (1981).

· · · · ·

· · · · ·

HALF A DOZEN MORE ETHNOGRAPHIES

After Nature: Marilyn Strathern, whose work on gender and exchange in Papua New Guinea is much admired, turns to English kinship in the twentieth century (1992).

Corn Is Our Blood: Alan Sandstrom's examination of Nahua (Aztec) theology and its relation to ethnic identity (1991).

The Golden Yoke: Rebecca French, who is both a lawyer and an anthropologist, gives a masterful account of Buddhist cosmology and its relationship to the traditional legal system of Tibet (1995).

Geisha: Liza Dalby trained as a geisha in Kyoto and provides a fascinating look at the "willow world" (1983).

This photograph of two geishas was probably taken between 1860 and 1930.

Persuasions of the Witch's Craft: Tanya Luhrman delves into the world of witches and magicians in contemporary Britain, exploring the implications of their beliefs in the context of modern society (1989).

Javanese Shadow Plays, Javanese Selves: Ward Keeler lived with a Javanese puppeteer for several years and wrote this fascinating account of an ancient art form, its practitioners, and its place in modern culture (1987).

This photograph, taken between 1900 and 1923, shows a Javanese shadow puppet play with musical accompaniment.

• • • • •

Dialogue is the backbone of ethnography. While anthropologists make use of a variety of techniques to elicit and record data, the interview is by far the most important. Interviews can range in formality from highly structured question-and-answer sessions with indigenous specialists, to the recording of life histories, to informal conversations, or to a chance exchange during an unanticipated encounter. Ultimately, the key to ethnographic success is *being there*, available to observe, available to follow up, available to take advantage of the chance event. Beyond the apparently simple techniques of interview and dialogue, ethnographers also employ a variety of more specialized techniques. Audio recording of speech and music, photography, film, drawing, genealogy, mapping, census taking, archival research, collecting material culture, collecting botanical or other natural samples, all have their ethnographic uses, depending on the ethnographer's specific research project.

Leaving the field can be almost as difficult as entering it: considering the effort required to establish oneself in a community, parting company with friends and now-familiar ways of life can be a wrenching experience. On an intellectual level, there are often nagging worries about whether one has really completed the research topic—a concern that is often justified. In a sense, no ethnographic research project is ever truly complete; it is always possible to learn more, to expand the temporal or spatial scope of one's understanding, or deepen the subtlety of that understanding. Epistemological misgivings, such as those discussed more fully in the next section, often bother the departing ethnographer. Nonetheless, a kind of closure is sometimes possible. Peter recalls relating his analysis of a particularly complex dispute to a friend who was one of the principal elders of Doro Ntika. His friend laughed, and slapping his thigh said, "You really *do* understand the way things work around here! Looks like you weren't wasting the past two years after all!"

Critiques of Ethnographic Fieldwork

For all its virtues, we would not want to give the impression that ethnographic fieldwork is the best method for all kinds of social science research, nor that participant observation is the only method employed by anthropologists. Fieldwork brings with it a substantial set of methodological and epistemological problems. Fieldwork also carries with it a unique set of ethical dilemmas.

The very strengths of classical ethnographic research have sometimes also proved to be weaknesses. One problem with participant observation has been a temptation for the ethnographer to present the community in a kind of temporal and spatial isolation. Many ethnographers, particularly in the "classic" accounts of the 1930s and 1940s, employed what came to be called the *ethnographic present*, in which communities were presented as frozen in time, outside any historical context, and without reference to neighboring societies or encapsulating states. For example, one of the most admired classics, Raymond Firth's *We the Tikopia*, described the social organization and traditional religion of the Tikopia without reference to the fact that half the population had recently converted to Christianity. Indeed, anthropologists may sometimes be carried away by the romance of their own enterprise and value the "unspoiled" traditions of a society far more than the people themselves do. A friend of ours visited Tikopia some twenty years after Firth had lived there, and was taken to a grotto by the sea where offerings to the gods of the old religion had been made. Seeing a single old offering, he asked his guide who had left it there, and was told "Fossi left it there." "Fossi," of course, is the Tikopia pronunciation of Firth's name. Ethnographers are not always successful in guarding against a temptation to romanticize the "otherness" of the people they study. Another criticism of the "ethnographic present" has concerned the tendency of ethnographers to write in an omniscient third-person voice, as if they had not been actively involved in eliciting the information they present. For better or worse, the past ten years has

One of the weaknesses of classical ethnographic research is the tendency of ethnographers to present their subjects as isolated in space and frozen in time, as New Zealand anthropologist Raymond Firth did in his study of the social organization and religious traditions of the people of Tikopia. The chiefs of Tikopia, a small island in the southwestern Pacific Ocean, one of the Solomon Islands, are depicted greeting the officers of the French exploration ship *Astrolabe* in this 1883 hand-colored lithograph of a work after Louis Auguste de Sanson.

seen the emergence of a genre of ethnography that seems as intent on conveying the ethnographer's personal experiences in collecting the data as in presenting the data themselves.

Participant observation—characterized by long-term intense interaction with relatively small groups of people—may allow the ethnographer to dig deeply into the complexities and subtleties of a community's social life. But how representative of larger social and cultural wholes can this be? Based on participant observation alone, it would be impossible for Peter to say to what extent the beliefs and values uncovered in the case of la Ninde are typical of the Dou Donggo in general, or of the regency of Bima, or of Indonesia, or of Southeast Asia. In approaching these problems we recall once again that ethnography is incomplete without the cross-cultural comparisons which allow the uniqueness of ethnographic description to find a comparative spatial and temporal context. Moreover, when it comes to matters of historicity and generalization, anthropologists often make use of the methods of allied disciplines such as history, psychology, and sociology.

There are also persistent questions about the "objectivity" of the data collected by means of participant observation. When a chemist sets out to analyze a sample, she might use a spectroscope. Like any scientific instrument, a spectroscope can be *calibrated* so that the scientist can be reasonably sure that data collected with one spectroscope will be comparable to data collected with a spectroscope calibrated in another time or place. But what—or, more appropriately, who—is the instrument of data collection in anthropology? Obviously, it is the ethnographer, and calibrating a human being is a far more daunting prospect than calibrating a spectroscope. Each ethnographer is a unique individual, the product of a unique upbringing and education, replete with all the psychological

Unlike an anthropologist, a spectroscope, an instrument designed for forming and examining optical spectra, may be calibrated so that data collected with one spectroscope will be comparable to data collected with another. In this photogravure from a painting by Richard Wimmer, German optician Joseph von Fraunhofer, the inventor of the spectroscope, demonstrates his creation.

predispositions—hidden as well as obvious—that constitute any human being. There have been notorious instances in which two anthropologists have studied the same community but come to very different conclusions about them. How, then, can we reconcile the inevitable subjectivity of participant observation with our desire for a calibrated uniformity of data collection? The short answer is that we can't, and it is this, more than anything else, that distinguishes social sciences such as anthropology from natural sciences such as chemistry, whatever their own problems of observer bias.

Can the problem of ethnographic subjectivity be overcome? The origins of participant observation as the hallmark method of anthropology began at the end of the last century as an attempt to compensate for the variable reliability of descriptions of non-Western peoples. Not content to rely on travelers' tales, missionary accounts, and official colonial reports of "customs and manners," W. H. R. Rivers, Bronislaw Malinowski, Franz Boas, and others among the founders of modern professional anthropology insisted on the firsthand collection of ethnographic data by trained observers. It was their hope that training would suffice to compensate for the prejudices of the observer. In the 1951 edition of the Royal Anthropological Institute's *Notes and Queries on Anthropology* the uninitiated were told that "amateurs untrained in anthropology . . . are apt to assume that they are free from bias. This, however, is far from the case; without a scientific training their observation will certainly be hampered by preconceived attitudes of mind." Standardized categories for data collection, such as those presented in *Notes and Queries* and the Human Relations Area Files' *Outline of Cultural Materials*, had been created in an attempt to overcome observer bias and ensure the comparability of data collected by different ethnographers. In the 1930s some American anthropologists even went so far as to undergo psychoanalysis before fieldwork in an attempt to "calibrate" the instrument of data collection, a practice quickly abandoned.

Other notable attempts to overcome these epistemological problems have included re-studies and studies undertaken by teams of ethnographers. One would think that a scientific approach to gathering ethnographic data would encourage anthropologists to re-study communities that had been studied before by other ethnographers as a check against subjectivity or bias. But this is far from common. To some extent this has been due to a sense of urgency among anthropologists to conduct *salvage ethnography*. Many have been concerned that most of the world's smaller societies and traditional ways of life are fast disappearing and that it is more important to record those that have never been studied than to confirm results already collected. It must also be admitted that many anthropologists were first attracted to the field by the romantic image of the lone, intrepid explorer, and that an unspoken ethnographic "machismo" has attached itself to those who have studied the previously unstudied. There has been, altogether, an understandable if misguided sense of proprietorship on the part of an ethnographer for "his" or "her people" which has made it very difficult for one ethnographer to "poach" on the "territory" of another. Finally, it has been rare for ethnographers working in communities that have been studied before to approach those communities interested in precisely the same theoretical or ethnographic issues as their predecessors. And because societies can change rapidly, separation in time of even a few years between an initial study and the next study also makes it difficult for re-studies to provide a check on ethnographic objectivity.

On occasion, anthropologists have engaged in the study of a particular community by a team of researchers, partly to provide greater comprehensiveness and partly to compensate for individual observer bias. The "Modjokuto Project" engaged seven social scientists (mostly anthropologists) in the study of a small town in central Java in the early 1950s, while the Mexican town of Zinacantan was serially the focus of scores of ethnographic studies in the 1960s and 1970s under the general supervision of Evon Vogt. Problems of funding and logistics make such projects difficult to organize and so they have been rare. Nonetheless, in some countries, notably Mexico and Japan, ethnographers are institutionally inclined to engage in team efforts, usually consisting of a group of advanced graduate students led by their professor. For all of this, it is not clear that the data collected by teams of ethnographers are significantly less subjective than those collected by groups.

More recently, some anthropologists have argued that "objectivity" is a false issue. Our bias—that is, our social and historical situation—is what gives us a point of view, and hence constitutes a resource we should openly draw upon in our interpretations. Others contend that any form of representation is an exercise in power and control. To these critics, the whole enterprise of ethnographic description is suspect so long as asymmetries of power persist between the observer and the observed. These critiques have occasioned new styles of ethnographic writing. In contrast to the language of omniscient objectivity that characterized earlier ethnography, some now favor the presentation of relatively unedited texts representing a variety of "voices" other than the ethnographer's. Other ethnographers have adopted the inclusion of a more autobiographical style of presentation, in which the ethnographer's background and relations with his or her subjects become a central topic of the ethnography. In a way, we may have come full circle back to travelers' tales. Unfortunately, few ethnographers have proved to be as interesting as the people they study.

All the same, isn't it an act of extraordinary hubris for someone to propose to present a definitive account of another people, even when it is based on long-term "participant observation"? And isn't it problematic that the vast majority of ethnographers are Westerners when the vast majority of their subjects have been non-Western? To some extent this is a self-correcting problem: more and more non-Western students are trained as anthropologists and more and more nations are developing their own traditions and styles of anthropological research. For example, most of the ethnography of Mexican communities is today written by Mexicans, in

Spanish, which was not the case twenty years ago. The same can be said to be true of gender: women, who now constitute a majority of recent doctorates in American anthropology, are frequently engaged in the study of women, both at home and elsewhere. By the same token, a number of non-Western ethnographers have begun to turn their attention to the study of Western societies. The discipline as a whole can only benefit from additional perspectives. After all, Alexis de Tocqueville's description of American society remains unsurpassed by any observation made by an American. In the same way, anthropologists have long regarded the "outsider's perspective" they bring to their subjects as one of the principal advantages of ethnographic method. A person studying his or her own culture can be likened to a fish trying to describe water. While the insider

French statesman and author
Alexis de Tocqueville's (1805–59) *Democracy in America* appeared in two volumes, in 1835 and 1840. This portrait of Tocqueville appeared in a book illustration in about 1901.

is capable of noticing subtle local variations, the outsider is far more likely to notice the tacit understandings that local people take for granted as "common sense" or "natural" categories of thought. The outsider status of the ethnographer, then, can be regarded as a strength as well as a weakness, even as a strength crucial to the success of the enterprise.

The Ethics of Ethnography

The nature of ethnographic work is such that the researcher develops a unique set of relationships with the people he or she studies, with host institutions and governments, and with colleagues. As anthropology has matured, the moral issues raised by these relationships have become matters of concern. Various professional associations have debated the issues and framed codes of ethical conduct. For fieldworkers the first imperative is to ensure that one's research does not harm the people one studies. For example, John and a colleague wrote a history of a Maya town in Guatemala. In a book review, a geographer questioned their expertise and political commitment by noting that the book failed to mention and criticize the establishment of an army garrison in the town in the 1980s. John and his colleague had certainly been aware of the army's presence (in 1979 a drunken soldier fired a machine gun into the house where John was sleeping). But John and his colleague declined to discuss the army in their book because, given the political situation in Guatemala at the time, and their close work with certain individuals and families in the town, critical mention of the army could have led to retaliation against their friends. Similarly, Peter's account of the case of la Ninde makes use of pseudonyms to protect the anonymity of the parties concerned—a fairly standard practice among anthropologists. Like other anthropologists, he also uses pseudonyms to refer to the places where he has worked.

A persistent source of ethical dilemma for ethnographers is to be found in the extent to which it is appropriate for ethnographers actively to influence the social, religious, or political life of the communities in which they work. In one celebrated case, for example, an ethnographer was presented with a situation in which members of her host community held the traditional belief that twins are inhuman and should be allowed to die of neglect. When twins were born to a village woman during her stay, she faced the dilemma of whether to intervene and if so, in what way. Should she try to persuade the mother not to abandon her newborn babies? Should she offer to adopt them herself? Should she inform village or government officials who disapproved of the traditional practice? Or, out of respect for the beliefs of her hosts, should she do nothing? For all our efforts to frame codes of professional behavior, there is no consensus among anthropologists as to how such dilemmas are to be resolved. Admittedly, most of the dilemmas anthropologists face are not matters of life and death, but the degree to which the participant observer should really participate in the affairs of the community remains a persistent and vexing problem. In a similar vein, John has frequently been asked by Mixtecs to aid them in entering the United States without a visa. How should he respond? On the one hand he feels a deep sense of obligation to people who have been his friends and hosts in Mexico. On the other hand, helping them in this way violates the laws of his own country.

At the same time, ethnographers have often felt compelled to become advocates for the people they study. The peoples anthropologists study have often been among those most vulnerable to colonial and neocolonial oppression, genocide, displacement, poverty, and general powerlessness in the face of governments and other institutions. Anthropologists sometimes (although hardly always) have access to media and other means of publicizing the plight of the people they study, and many have made use of this access. Advocacy has not been without risk to these anthropologists, who have suffered deportation, imprisonment, and even assassination in retaliation for their actions.

One ethical issue that has received increasing attention concerns intellectual property rights. Anthropologists have been criticized for "profiting" from the "expropriation" of indigenous cultural knowledge. Are indigenous peoples entitled to copyright knowledge that has traditionally been in the public domain? Should communities be able to exercise control over the publication of cultural knowledge? Should they be entitled to pass binding editorial judgment on the interpretations ethnographers make? Are ethnographers obliged to share what profits, if any, they make from the sale of ethnographic accounts with the subjects of their accounts?

Ultimately, we have to confront more general ethical issues. To whom does an ethnographer owe his or her greatest allegiance? Is it to the people studied, to the sovereign government of the country where research takes place, to the agency or foundation that funds the ethnographer's research, to the academic or research institution that employs the ethnographer, or to the community of scholars to which the ethnographer belongs? Should ethnographers be expected only to add to humanity's knowledge of itself or should they be expected to provide more tangible benefits to the people they study or to the world at large? Should ethnographers be held to a higher standard than the one applied to journalists, filmmakers, or photographers who also report on their fellow human beings? These, too, are unresolved questions, subject to lively debate.

What can we expect of ethnography and the ethnographer? For all of the claims made for and against the products of participant observation, anthropology has always relied on what amounts to a good-faith effort on the part of ethnographers to tell their stories as fully and honestly as possible. Similarly, we have relied on the common decency of ethnographers to act with due regard for the integrity of their profession. We all recognize that complete descriptive objectivity is impossible, that a comprehensive understanding of any society or culture is unattainable, and that ethical problems are more easily posed than resolved. That we continue to pose these questions is perhaps the best indication of the fundamental health of anthropology as both an academic discipline and a humanistic enterprise.

TWO

Bee Larvae and Onion Soup: Culture

•

When I consider Thy heavens, the work of Thy fingers, the moon and the
stars, which Thou hast ordained;
What is Man, that Thou art mindful of him? and the son of Man, that
Thou visitest him?
For Thou hast made him a little lower than the angels, and hast crowned
him with glory and honor.
Thou madest him to have dominion over the works of Thy hands; Thou
hast put all things under his feet:
All sheep and oxen, yea, and the beasts of the field;
The fowl of the air, and the fish of the sea, and whatsoever passeth through
the paths of the seas.

Psalm 8:3–8

Most anthropologists agree that culture has to do with the aspects of human knowledge and activity
that people learn as members of a society. This photograph, taken in 1939, shows a dance instructor
training a young child in traditional Balinese dance. Gamelan musicians accompany the lessons.

Even if we take the psalmist's triumphalism with a grain of salt, it is hard to deny that *Homo sapiens* is an unusual species in the natural history of this planet. Other species are faster, stronger, better adapted to their environments by physique and instinct than we are. What is it, then, that separates our species from all others? There are many things about humans that are unique. But perhaps the most extraordinary characteristic is our capacity to conceptualize the world and to communicate those conceptions symbolically. Anthropologists, especially those trained in the American tradition, call this capacity "culture."

What Is "Culture"?

However we define culture, most anthropologists agree that it has to do with those aspects of human cognition and activity that are derived from what we learn as members of society, keeping in mind that one learns a great deal that one is never explicitly taught. Indeed, no species has as protracted a period of infantile and juvenile dependence, a period that allows for and is devoted to the absorption and transmission of ways of knowing and doing, ways that are unique to each society. It is impossible to imagine anything beyond even a rudimentary technology—such as one based on the manufacture of stone tools—in the absence of an exceptional capacity to conceptualize abstract ideas and communicate them symbolically, the primary human means for which is, of course, language. Our genetically inherited predisposition for language and symbolic communication, and all of the complex social organization that it makes possible, has allowed the human race to achieve a kind of inheritance of acquired characteristics in which the acquisition of knowledge can be cumulative from generation to generation.

We hasten to add that there have probably been more anthropological definitions of *culture* than there have been anthropologists. The two of us were trained with a sense of culture as "shared patterns of learned behavior." In the Victorian era, Edward B. Tylor's 1871 definition of culture endured essentially unchallenged for thirty years: "Culture or civilization, taken in its wide [comparative] ethnographic sense, is that complex whole which includes knowledge, belief, art, morals, law, custom, and any other capabilities and habits acquired by man as a member of society." Tylor's focus on knowledge and belief as acquired—that is, *learned*—by members of a social group, as well as his sense that these constitute an integrated system, continue to inform our sense of what culture is. On the other hand, the Victorians tended to regard "culture or civilization" as something a nation or people might possess to a greater or less degree. In this sense of the term, the fellow who goes to the opera, sips champagne, and reads Proust is more "cultured" than the one who goes to a soccer match, swills beer, and reads the tabloid dailies. While this sense may continue in everyday uses of the term "culture," it is rejected by anthropologists.

· · · · ·

Culture, or civilization . . . is that complex whole which includes knowledge, belief, art, morals, law, custom, and any other capabilities and habits acquired by man as a member of society.

Edward Tylor, 1871

· · · · ·

That rejection of the term *culture* as something that a people or an individual has more or less of has profoundly changed the way the modern world views differences between societies. Returning to

Cambridge from World War II, Raymond Williams found himself "preoccupied by a single word, *culture*." Where he had previously heard the term used to refer to "a kind of social superiority" or "where it was an active word for writing poems and novels, making films and paintings, working in theatres," he now heard it in a sense that indicated "powerfully but not explicitly, some central formation of values" as well as "a use which made it almost equivalent to *society*: a particular *way of life*—"American culture," "Japanese culture." Williams was hearing the rippling consequences of a rethinking of the culture concept at the turn of the century by German and American social theorists, most prominently Franz Boas.

Franz Boas is generally considered the father of modern American cultural anthropology. Born in Germany in 1858, Boas was trained at the universities of Heidelberg, Bonn, and Kiel, concentrating in his studies on geography and what was called "psychophysics," which focused on the study of how the characteristics of the observer determined the perception of physical phenomena. At the same time, as a Jew he was alienated from the politics and social establishments of nineteenth-century Germany, which was one of the reasons for his emigration to the United States six years after completing

The father of modern American cultural anthropology, German American anthropologist Franz Boas (1858–1942), pictured here in a photograph taken in 1906, was fascinated by the idea that environment had a determining effect on how one views the world.

his doctorate. From the outset, Boas was fascinated by the idea that environment, cultural as well as physical, had a determining effect on the way one views the world. His earliest work in "psychophysics" had to do with the way Eskimos (Inuit) perceived and categorized the color of seawater. After several years Boas received an appointment at Columbia University in New York, which became the principal training ground for the next two generations of American anthropologists.

Boas' earliest work, *The Central Eskimo*, published in 1888, dealt with the way Inuit people perceived and categorized the color of seawater. This photograph, taken sometime between 1910 and 1925, shows a group of Inuit men spearfishing for salmon in an ocean inlet.

. . . . .

Culture embraces all the manifestations of social behaviour of a community, the reactions of the individual as affected by the habits of the group in which he lives, and the product of human activities as determined by these habits.

Franz Boas, 1930

. . . . .

Where Tylor saw "culture" as an accumulation of human accomplishment, Boas described a "*Kulturbrille*," a set of "cultural glasses" that each of us wears, lenses that provide us with a means for perceiving the world around us, for interpreting the meaning of our social lives, and framing action in them. Here is something that happened to John during a stay with the Mixtec of Oaxaca, Mexico:

I was invited to go hunting with several of my Mixtec friends. We hadn't had much luck, only managing to shoot a couple of thin squirrels. Toward the end of the day I was following my friends up the side of a ridge. They were well ahead of me, and when I finally reached the top I could see them crouched around something at the base of a tree and talking excitedly. As I approached, I saw it was a beehive, which one of them knocked down with a stick. When it hit the ground it split open, revealing a mass of comb, honey, and bee larvae. My three friends were busy tearing out pieces of the hive—including those containing the bee larvae—and popping them into their mouths. One of them suddenly stood up and said, "Wait, we're being impolite." He reached down into the hive and pulled out a big glob of comb, honey, and squiggling bee larvae. He then turned to me and said, while holding out his hand, "Here John, this is all for you." Seeing no way to refuse him I took it from him, held my breath, put it in my mouth and swallowed.

About a year later I got a revenge of sorts when I invited some of the same people over to my house to eat. As a surprise I prepared onion soup, something I am partial to but had never seen served anywhere in Oaxaca. After serving out the portions, I noticed that my guests were slow to begin eating. Then, out of the corner of my eye, I saw one of my hunting companions pour his bowl out onto the dirt floor behind a table. When I asked if there was something wrong they at

This recent photograph provides an up-close view of bees and their larvae in a honeycomb.

first refused to say anything until one finally, with a disgusted look on his face said, "Onions have a terrible odor and, if you eat too much of them it makes you stupid!"

What has this mutual disgust at each other's eating habits got to do with culture? For one thing, it shows that both Americans and the Mixtec make a distinction between "food" and "not-food" in ways that have to do with more than simple considerations of edibility. Insects are in fact not just edible, they are quite nutritious, and onions contain lots of vitamins. This kind of categorization is part of the work of culture, and it is something that we do not only with regard to food, but in every other imaginable domain. John's disgust arose because he had learned to categorize insects as "vermin" (definitely not food), while his Mixtec friends were disgusted by onion soup because they had learned to classify onions as a "condiment," and no more suitable for a meal than a bowl of mustard would be for us and, taken in excess, positively stupefying. But perhaps more to the point—and here we return to Boas' metaphor of "cultural glasses"—experience is not simply given to us. For John and his Mixtec friends, eating is something that is part of a complex system of ideas, perceptions, norms, values, feelings, and behaviors so that the act of eating is never just about satisfying hunger, but is also an expression of how we have learned to see the world. Culture, like a set of glasses, focuses our experience of the world. And as this example shows, culture becomes a part of us, right down to "natural" reactions, such as nausea. Over the years John has dined on grasshoppers, grubs, flying ants, and other, unnamed, insects; Mixtec cuisine is far from crude or primitive—an entire culinary aesthetic has developed based on foodstuffs Westerners consider "inedible." We may know in a dispassionate intellectual sense that insects are good for you, but John, at least, can never bring himself to feel completely at ease when eating a bug. (Peter can report similar experiences with goat testicles.)

· · · · ·

Culture is the integral whole consisting of implements and consumers' goods, of constitutional charters for the various social groupings, of human ideas and crafts, beliefs and customs. Whether we consider a very simple or primitive culture or an extremely complex and developed one, we are confronted by a vast apparatus, partly material, partly human, and partly spiritual, by which man is able to cope with the concrete, specific problems that face him.

Bronislaw Malinowski, 1944

· · · · ·

John's experience provides a good way of looking at how anthropologists have used the idea of culture to uncover some of the fundamental ways learned behavior shapes our lives and how they have begun to understand the ways in which, to paraphrase Clyde Kluckhohn, each person is simultaneously like some other people, like all other people, and like no other person. In John's story our attention is immediately attracted to the exotic, to the seemingly bizarre tastes of the Mixtec, in short, to the *differences* cultures make between peoples. But the story could equally be read for what it reveals about the *similarities* between John and the Mixtec, similarities that may be part of a universal human heritage. For example, as we noted above, both Americans and the Mixtec employ an elaborate system of *classification* to deal with food. The specific content of the categories may differ, but the fact of classification remains constant. Indeed, the universal propensity of humans to create systems of classification, by means of which categorical meaning is assigned to domains as disparate as foodstuffs, diseases, and colors, has long been a subject of fascination and debate among anthropologists.

At the beginning of this century, the French social theorist Émile Durkheim and his nephew Marcel Mauss argued that the human capacity for classification was an extension of our social nature. "Society was not simply a model which classificatory thought followed; it was its own divisions which served as divisions for the system of classification. The first logical categories were social categories; the first classes of things were classes of men, into which these things were integrated." Half a century later, Claude Lévi-Strauss, the founder of "structuralist" anthropology, would claim that human classification is indeed universal, but that it is universal because a human predisposition to making distinctions produced classifications that mutatis mutandis were but surface representations of a more fundamental "deep structure" shaped by the binary nature of the human mind: "[I]f we look at all the intellectual undertakings of mankind . . . the common denominator is always to introduce some kind of order. If this represents a basic need for

French social theorist Émile Durkheim (1858–1917), shown here in an undated photograph, argued that the human capacity for classification was an extension of our social nature.

order in the human mind and since, after all, the human mind is only part of the universe, the need probably exists because there is some order in the universe and the universe is not chaos."

. . . . .

Culture is neither natural nor artificial. It stems from neither genetics nor rational thought, for it is made up of rules of conduct, which were not invented and whose function is generally not understood by the people who obey them. Some of these rules are residues of traditions acquired in the different types of social structure through which . . . each human group has passed. Other rules have been consciously accepted or modified for the sake of specific goals. Yet there is no doubt that, between the instincts inherited from our genotype and the rules inspired by reason, the mass of unconscious rules remains more important and more effective; because reason itself . . . is a product rather than a cause of cultural evolution.

Claude Lévi-Strauss, 1983

. . . . .

In the United States, an interest in native systems of classification led in the 1960s to an approach that came to be called "ethnoscience," in which formal methods of analysis were applied to domains such as kinship terms, flora and fauna, color, diseases, and the like. One observation that came out of ethnoscience was that while the content of cultural categories was plastic, arbitrary, and highly variable, that variability was itself both ordered and constrained by, among other things, the physiological means of perception. More recently yet,

French philosopher Michel Foucault (1926–84), shown here in a photograph taken in 1979, popularized a new direction among some anthropologists that sees the categories of meaning imposed by culture as a basis of inequality and oppression.

the French philosopher Michel Foucault has popularized a new direction among some anthropologists, who have come to see the categories of meaning imposed by culture as a basis of inequality and oppression. In other words, they see the ability to control the content of cultural classifications as a primary source of power in society. This in turn makes the *contestation* of categories of social classification, such as "male" and "female," with all of the social, political, and economic associations that attend them, a primary mode of resistance to authority.

Going back to our example of John's experience with his Mixtec friends, it is of course difficult to see how classifying onions as a meal or a condiment has much to do with power. Indeed, not all of what we do is motivated politically, and in behavior associated with such an important area as food, moral precepts (as expressed in the etiquette of serving guests first and with choice portions) are at least as significant as considerations of dominance and resistance. This, too, is something we can see as informative about the similarities that unite human cultures even as our differences can divide us. The behavior that John recounts in his story is not random, nor can it be described purely by the logic of economic utility. The whole notion of etiquette, of manners, if you like, is one shared by all human cultures. Eating is not simply the satisfaction of our need for nutrition: it is hedged about with a *system* of conceptual categories (e.g., "food" vs. "nonfood" or "choice" vs. "ordinary" items), moral values (e.g., favoring one's guest), and culturally determined emotions (e.g., delight or disgust) which invest the satisfaction of nutritional needs with meanings that give it depth and resonance as a human experience.

· · · · ·

Culture lends significance to human experience by selecting from and organizing it. It refers broadly to the forms throughout which people make sense of their lives . . . It does not inhabit a set-aside domain, as does . . . politics or economics. From the pirouettes of classical ballet to the most brute of brute facts, all human conduct is

culturally mediated. Culture encompasses the everyday and the eso-
teric, the mundane and the elevated, the ridiculous and the sublime.
Neither high nor low, culture is all-pervasive.

Renato Rosaldo, 1989

· · · · ·

Human cultures, then, seem to be infinitely variable, but in fact
that variability takes place within the boundaries produced by physical
and mental capacities. Human languages, for example, are tremendously
diverse, differing in sound, grammar, and semantics. But all are dependent
upon what appears to be a uniquely human capacity and predisposition for
learning languages. While the range of sounds used in human languages
extends from clicks and pops to guttural stops, the distinctive speech sounds
that are meaningful in all the languages of the world are but a fraction of
the sounds it is possible for humans to make. Another way that we might
observe the intricate relationship between the culturally specific and the
universal is in the way John and his Mixtec friends reacted emotionally, even
viscerally, to bee larvae and onion soup: whether they felt delight or disgust
was determined by the way they had learned to perceive food, but delight
and disgust seem to be basic and universal human reactions to food.

Where Is Culture?

At least three points of debate have continued to recur in the way
anthropologists talk about the concept of culture. One has to do with the
extent to which a "culture" should be regarded as an integrated whole;
the second has to do with the extent to which "culture" can be seen as an
autonomous, "superorganic" entity; and the third has to do with how we
can best go about drawing boundaries around "cultures."

The idea that culture is an integrated and integrating whole is in part based upon the great modernist insight that underlying apparently discrete bits of belief or behavior rests a more fundamental reality. For Karl Marx that determining reality was the mode of production; for Émile Durkheim it was society; for Sigmund Freud it was the unconscious; and for many in anthropology, following the lead of Boas, it has been culture itself. Different schools within anthropology have formed around ideas about the nature of this whole. Ruth Benedict, one of Boas' first students, conceived of a culture as a *Gestalt*, a total pattern. In her classic work, *Patterns of Culture*, Benedict compared beliefs and institutions across several societies, noting how differences between cultures were consistent within a single culture. In other words, Benedict felt that the practices, beliefs, and values of a given culture differed from other cultures in a consistent and mutually reinforcing way. She could thus characterize the Zuñi (southwest United States) as "Apollonian," the Kwakiutl (northwest coast of North America) as "Dionysian," and the Dobu (southwest Pacific) as "paranoid schizophrenic." Although Benedict's approach is now regarded as too simplistic and reductionist, because of its tendency to view cultures in terms of one or two key themes, it has continued to prove a powerful means for organizing and integrating the minutiae of ethnographic observation. Clifford Geertz is one contemporary anthropologist who has been spectacularly adept with this approach: in one classic description of Balinese society, for example, he used cockfighting—a popular form of entertainment in Bali—as an image that also serves to characterize beliefs and practices ranging from the way Balinese men see their sexual potency to the way status hierarchies organize the whole society. In this way, Geertz is able to show how disparate elements of Balinese culture create a "fabric of meaning and belief" that is consistent and mutually reinforcing. For

American anthropologist Clifford Geertz (1926–2006) used cockfighting, a popular form of
entertainment in Bali, as an image that also helped to characterize beliefs and practices ranging
from the way Balinese men see their sexual potency to the way status hierarchies organize the whole
society. This 1939 photograph shows a large crowd in Bali waiting for a cockfight to begin.

Geertz, cultures can be read as texts, much as one might read a novel or a
poem. The trick, according to Geertz, is to seek out cultural "texts" that
the people of the society themselves find compelling—as the Balinese are
fascinated by cockfighting—and not only to understand them as they see
them, but to see the ways the themes of these "texts" illuminate other
aspects of the society.

Another view of integration has a more rationalistic basis, derived as it is from the linguistic idea of a grammar or set of rules underlying speech. In this approach, culture is often spoken of as a code or program. Thus, culture is integrated by the internal logic of the rules that enable it to be meaningful and productive. Hence, the American anthropologist Ward Goodenough uses the example of a football game to illustrate the goal of ethnographic description. If you want to play football you need to learn enough of the rules and style of playing the game to get along with the other players. By analogy an ethnographer should aspire to learn enough of the social rules and customs of a culture to be able to live in a way acceptable to the people he or she studies.

· · · · ·

Culture, then, consists of standards for deciding what is, standards for deciding what can be, standards of deciding how one feels about it, standards for deciding what to do about it, and standards for deciding how to go about doing it.

Ward H. Goodenough, 1963

· · · · ·

A third concept of integration draws on the notion of a formal system, where elements stand in a relationship of mutual implication. Robert Murphy once observed: "Simple though it is, the idea that societies are systematized is central to the social sciences. The systematization occurs through the mutual adjustment of norms, ideas, values, aesthetics, and other things cultural, and it takes place in the arena of practical, everyday activity, in the adaptation and accommodation to each other of ways of behaving." For example, in

In *Pigs for the Ancestors* (1968), Roy Rappaport (1926–97) described a complex ecological system in Highland New Guinea in which elaborate ritual cycles regulate the size of the domestic pig population. This photograph, taken in 1949, shows a New Guinean man watching pigs feed.

Pigs for the Ancestors, Roy Rappaport illustrated a complex ecological system in which the elaborate ritual cycles of the Tsembaga Maring of Highland New Guinea operate as a self-balancing mechanism that regulates the size of the domestic pig population, acreage under cultivation, fallow periods, energy expenditure, subsistence activities, diet, and intertribal warfare.

At the opposite extreme are those who would deny that culture is integrated, or at least to the extent implied in the foregoing examples. Early studies of the borrowing or diffusion of traits among Native Americans led Robert Lowie, another student of Boas, to suggest that culture is nothing more than "a thing of shreds and patches," the product of a complex but essentially random history. A rejoinder to this critique was provided by Claude Lévi-Strauss, who pointed out that although the elements found in a given culture might have a wide range of historical origins, they have been pieced together as a "*bricolage*," a kind of collage in which the odds and ends of culture are turned to uses for which they may never have been intended but which fit into an underlying pattern. More recently, anthropologists who reject the modernist assumption of underlying foundations have appropriated the idea of *bricolage* to view the essence of culture as a constant reworking, casting off, and reviving of elements into ever-changing complexes. This allows them to avoid the problem of essentializing culture, that is, treating it as if it exists outside of history and not subject to human agency.

Up to this point we have taken the collective nature of culture for granted. In fact we often refer to cultures as if they were autonomous things with lives of their own. Alfred Kroeber once compared culture to a coral reef, which is built up by the secretions of millions of tiny animals, but which existed before any of its living members, and will outlast them all, providing a structure within which future generations will be constrained. In using this metaphor Kroeber explicitly minimized the role of individuals in shaping social and historical trends. Yet if culture consists of what we learn as members of society, it would seem that culture must be located in human heads. But isn't it true, as the Mexican proverb states, "*Cada cabeza es un mundo*" (Each mind is a different world)? And how accessible can the contents of an individual mind be to an ethnographer? Anthony Wallace argued that the contents of the individual mind are in fact highly divergent, and that what culture does is not so much impose a uniformity, but provide a set of shared communicative symbols that organizes this diversity.

• • • • •

Culture means the whole complex of traditional behaviour which has been developed by the human race and is successively learned by each generation. A culture is less precise. It can mean the forms of traditional behaviour which are characteristic of a given society, or of a group of societies, or of a certain race, or of a certain area, or of a certain period of time.

Margaret Mead, 1937

• • • • •

The indeterminacy that is built into the concept of culture would seem to make it difficult, even with physically isolated peoples, to determine precisely where one culture ends and another begins. One of the deep roots of the Boasian concept of culture after all was the German concern with nation building. In the eighteenth and nineteenth centuries Germany was divided into a number of different kingdoms and

The Boasian concept of culture was to some extent rooted in the German concern with nation building. Germany was divided into different kingdoms and principalities until the proclamation of the German Empire in the Hall of Mirrors at Versailles in 1871. This map, which was published in *The Historical Atlas* by William R. Shepherd in 1923, shows eighteenth-century divisions in the Wurtemberg region of Germany, including duchies, ecclesiastical domains, imperial cities, counties, and other secular lordships.

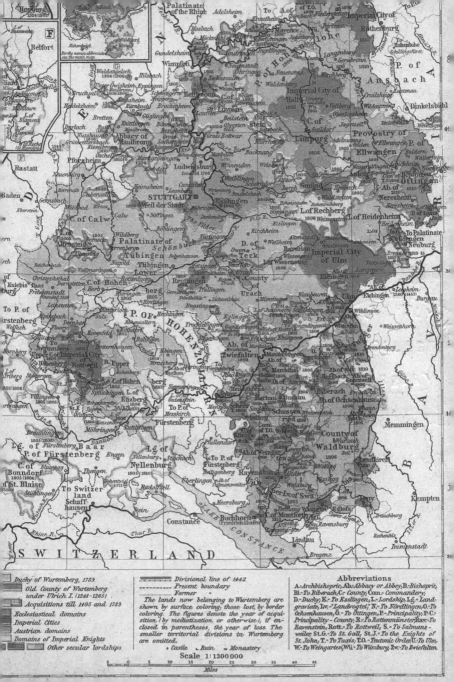

WÜRTEMBERG

Legend

- Duchy of Wurtemberg, 1789
- Old County of Wurtemberg under Ulrich I. (1244–1265)
- Acquisitions till 1495 and 1789
- Ecclesiastical domains
- Imperial Cities
- Austrian domains
- Domains of Imperial Knights
- Other secular lordships

• Castle   ⌂ Ruin   ⬚ Monastery

Divisional lines

——— Divisional line of 1442
--------- Present boundary
————— Former

The lands now belonging to Wurtemberg are shown by surface coloring; those lost, by border coloring. The figures denote the year of acquisition (by mediatization, or otherwise); if enclosed in parentheses, the year of loss. The smaller territorial divisions in Wurtemberg are omitted.

Scale 1:1300000

Miles

Abbreviations

A.=Archbishopric, Ab.=Abbacy or Abbey, B.=Bishopric, Bi.=To Biberach, C.= County, Com.= Commandery; D.=Duchy, E.= To Esslingen, L.=Lordship, Lg.= Landgraviate, Lw.="Landvogtei, N.= To Nördlingen, O.=To Ochsenhausen, Ö.= To Ottingen, P.=Principality, P.C.=Principality- County, R.=To Rottenmünster, Rav.=To Ravenstein, Rott.=To Rottweil, S.=To Salmans-weiler, St.G.=To St. Gall, St.J.=To the Knights of St. John, T.=To Taxis, T.O.=Teutonic Order, U.=To Ulm, W.=To Weingarten, Wü.=To Würzburg, Zw.=To Zwiefalten.

principalities. Nationalists employed the idea of a Pan-German *Kultur* or *Geist*, to argue that German people shared a great deal (language, folklore, and customs among other things) and this *Kultur* or *Geist* transcended the political divisions separating them. This premise, combined with the essentialism attributed to culture, found itself expressed in ethnographies that routinely assumed "one people, one culture, one society." But, as Arjun Appadurai recently asked, doesn't this premise fly in the face of "unequal knowledge and the differential prestige of lifestyles, and discourage attention to the world views and agency of those who are marginalized or dominated"? Perhaps it would be best to join with most anthropologists today, who tend to view culture not as a thing in itself, but as a learning device for uncovering meaning in social life. In this respect one is more likely to read in ethnographies specific discussions of norms, values, beliefs, ontologies, worldview, ideologies, and categories that may in fact be seriously contested than totalizing statements about such and such a "culture." In addition, a number of anthropologists have concerned themselves with developing concepts that transcend the pervasive dualisms that have informed many of our debates about the nature of culture. One example is the idea of "embodiment," that is, when we act, we act not simply as minds but also as physical bodies. Thus when John consumes insects in the Mixteca he not only thinks "bugs are vermin" but viscerally experiences bugs as vermin.

It might be said that, whatever its difficulties, the anthropological concept of culture has been our discipline's most significant contribution to modern thought. In uncovering the fundamentally arbitrary and learned basis for the differences among and between human communities, the culture concept has been a powerful weapon in combating racism, national chauvinism, and the "scientific" racism that characterized much of anthropology in the nineteenth century. For Boas and his students, fighting racism and ethnocentrism—the tendency to measure others entirely by the yardstick of one's own values—was a primary mission for the discipline of anthropology. Ever the empiricist, Boas carried out studies that countered prevalent American beliefs in the hereditary "weakness" and "inferiority" of certain immigrant nationalities by showing that once in the United States improved conditions of health and nutrition quickly produced populations as robust as any. Boas' conviction that environment rather than biological inheritance is the principal determinant of character and behavior in humans was taken up by some of his students and developed into a theory of cultural determinism that reached a crescendo in the "nature versus nurture" debates that still engage us.

Cultural Relativism

Among the moral, philosophical, and political consequences of the emergence of the concept of culture has been the development of a doctrine of *cultural relativism*. We start from the premise that our beliefs, morals, behaviors—even our very perceptions of the world around us—are the products of culture, learned as members of the communities in which we are reared. If, as we believe, the content of culture is the product of the arbitrary, historical experience of a people, then what we are as social beings is also an arbitrary, historical product. Because culture so deeply and broadly determines our worldview, it stands to reason that we can have no objective basis for asserting that one such worldview is superior to another, or that one worldview can be used as a yardstick to measure another. In this sense, cultures can be judged only *relative* to one another, and the meaning of a given belief or behavior must first and foremost be understood relative to its own cultural context. That, in a nutshell, is the basis of what has come to be called *cultural relativism*.

It is important to understand that many anthropologists, especially in the United States, regard relativism not as a dogma or an ideological desideratum, but, at heart, as an empirical finding. This has been most prominently expressed in the work of the anthropological linguists Edward Sapir and Benjamin Lee Whorf, who used linguistic data to show that categories such as time, space, and number are given in different ways by different languages, leading Sapir to state that in learning a language, we learn a world. Thus, when reporting on a cloudburst speakers of English are likely to say "it is raining." But what is the "it" that is raining? We say "it is raining" because we are predisposed by our language to think of events in the world in terms of the direct effects of specific causes. In contrast, an Indonesian would report "*Ada hujan*" ("there is rain"). Rather than cause and effect, the Indonesian expression predisposes its speakers toward seeing the world as a flowing together of things and events.

Taken to an extreme, a view of relativism that consigns the members of different cultures to utterly different worlds would make all translation impossible, including the translation performed in ethnography. As Dan Sperber has observed, "the relativist slogan, that people of different cultures live in different worlds, would be nonsense if understood as literally referring to physical worlds," and an extreme "relativist in earnest should be either quite pessimistic about the possibility of doing ethnography at all or extraordinarily optimistic about the abilities of ethnographers." What cognitive relativism does mean is that the orientations provided in a language have consequences for a range of beliefs, institutions, and behaviors, something we should expect if cultures are even imperfectly integrated wholes. In the Indonesian example we might note that a predisposition toward viewing events in the world as confluences rather than as the immediate effects of causes is consistent with holding a person legally liable for events they "might have" caused, as was the case in the anecdote recounted in the last chapter.

In addition to these aspects of cultural relativism we must also entertain the moral dimensions of cultural relativism. If the way one perceives the world is a product of one's culture, then even more so are the beliefs, values, and social norms that govern one's behavior. On what basis, then, can any one society claim a monopoly on moral truth or claim to have discovered a superior set of norms and values? Behavior that might be nonsensical, illegal, or immoral in one society might be perfectly rational and socially accepted in another. The only reasonable thing to do, it would seem, is to suspend any judgment of the practices of another society. But this is not as simple a matter as it may seem to be. For one thing, we immediately reencounter the problem of determining where cultural boundaries might be drawn, a particularly difficult matter in today's world in which global patterns of migration and diaspora have led to the possibility of truly multicultural societies. How do we deal with the stranger in our midst when that stranger's culture is morally different from our own? At what point are segments of a given community entitled to a claim of cultural distinctiveness that demands autonomy and respect? Are soccer hooligans or terrorists entitled to claim the protection of cultural relativism? Must we in the name of cultural relativism refrain from acting against ancient and traditional cultural practices in others that we see as oppressing a segment or class of that society?

• • • • •

Culture is . . . learned, adaptable, symbolic behaviour, based on a full-
fledged language, associated with technical inventiveness, a complex
of skills that in turn depends on a capacity to organize exchange relationships between communities.

Adam Kuper, 1994

• • • • •

This is not merely an abstract metaphysical problem. Take
the practice of female circumcision as one example of this sort of
dilemma. In a number of East African societies it has long been the
practice to mark a girl's passage to womanhood with, among other
things, a genital operation that in its most extreme form includes the
unanesthetized excision of the clitoris and labia. It is easy to see this
practice as violating basic human rights and equally easy to be moved
to work for its suppression. On the other hand, doing so would be a
fundamental violation of the cultural autonomy of the people who
practice this ritual. Moreover, when, as cognitive relativism dictates,
we view the practice in the context of cultural theories regarding
sexuality, reproduction, gender, and the life cycle, we may find, as
Janice Boddy did in her study of the Hofriyati of Northern Sudan,
that female circumcision participates with male circumcision in a
rich set of meanings having to do with the way society, rather than
nature, makes boys and girls into men and women. Placed in its
cultural context, Hofriyati female circumcision is neither irrational
nor deliberately cruel and oppressive and is, moreover, a practice
as much subscribed to by traditional Hofriyati women as men. We

may find the consequences of such practices repellent, but we are hard-pressed to find a moral basis for advocating its suppression that does not also violate the cultural autonomy of the Hofriyati. One wonders, ultimately, if it is logically possible to simultaneously subscribe to both the notion of universal human rights and a belief in the relativity of cultures.

For all these problems, we note with Clifford Geertz that the crimes committed in the name of cultural relativism pale in comparison to those committed in the name of cultural and national chauvinism or, for that matter, almost any other "ism." His stance is one of "anti-anti-relativism" and is a position we find congenial. One can make a claim for meddling in the business of others on the basis of a common humanity; we do, after all, share this planet as a single species. But any such claim should be made with the greatest care and reluctance, and only after a sincere and thorough attempt to understand what it is we object to in its own cultural context.

PEOPL

WE

PASS

Stories of Lif
among the Masse
of New York City

By

Julian Ralph

Illustrated

THREE

A Brief Encounter: Society

•

IMAGINE YOURSELF MEETING A stranger for the first time—the person in the next seat on a train, perhaps, or someone at a party. The conversation that ensues tends to be a pretty predictable one: What's your name? Where are you from? What do you do? What friends, business associates, or relatives might we have in common? Where did you go to school? It's a familiar set of questions. If the conversation is between members of the opposite sex, and things seem to be proceeding smoothly, one might look for conversational clues to determine if the other person is married, or "involved" with someone.

Naturally, as we are human beings rather than automatons, the course of such conversations is not entirely predictable, but can turn to topics

When we converse with someone upon first meeting, what we are trying to do is determine our conversational partner's class, ethnic origin, marital status, and other relevant characteristics, for as much as we would like to think otherwise, we are not purely unique and autonomous individuals but derive many facets of our identity from the various groups to which we belong. This 1896 advertisement for Julian Ralph's book *People We Pass* was created by Edward Penfield.

of mutual interest—sports, food, music, current events, and the like—and will be more or less awkward or pleasant depending on individual preferences and styles. Similarly, the stock set of questions one tends to ask will vary from one part of the world to another. For example, in the United States one's religion is regarded as a relatively private matter, while in Indonesia it is quite acceptable to ask a person's religion. But let us take a step back, and ask ourselves, what kind of information about someone do we tend to seek out first. And why?

What we are trying to do, as painlessly and efficiently as etiquette allows, is to determine our interlocutor's class, ethnic origin, marital status, and other relevant characteristics. Such questions allow us to determine what we can expect from our interlocutor, and predict what he or she expects from us. It allows us to determine what will be appropriate topics of conversation. It allows us to discover whether and in what ways the other person will be useful to us. Why is that? It is because people are not purely unique and autonomous individuals, no matter how much we would like to think of ourselves that way. We derive many facets of our identity from the various groups to which we belong.

In the last chapter we discussed the ways in which anthropologists view behavior as an outcome of mental maps provided to us by culture. But it is important to recognize that human behavior is also an aspect of our nature as members of a *social* species. As everyone knows, we are organized into groups whose internal and external relations are governed by *rules*, perform a variety of *functions*, and which endure beyond the lives of their constituent members. We may *have* a culture, but we *belong to* a society. In other words, an interest in culture is prompted by a desire to discover the way people comprehend the world around them, to frame their action, and to interpret the actions of others. An interest in society has more to do with understanding the rules and regularities that govern human social behavior, the ways people associate with one another, and how activity is organized. These two approaches are far from incompatible; they are simply different angles from which to see the same complex thing.

Structure and Function

One of the things our symbol-making capacity enables us to do is organize ourselves in complex and subtle ways. Perhaps the most fundamental way in which human groups arrange themselves is through a division of labor. Indeed, anthropologists have historically differentiated societies based on the complexity of this division of labor, with even the most technologically simple societies assigning tasks to people on the basis of age and gender. Implicit in this view is the notion that groups are formed to accomplish particular functions and that they coordinate their activities with other groups.

· · · · ·

BRONISLAW MALINOWSKI (1884–1942)

A Founder of Modern Social Anthropology

Born in Poland, Bronislaw Malinowski began his studies in the natural sciences first in Kraków and then in Leipzig, where he studied under Max Wilhelm Wundt, who had also taught Franz Boas and Émile Durkheim. In 1910 he went to the London School of Economics and in due course received a grant to study the people of the Trobriand Islands, which lie off the southeastern coast of Papua New Guinea. As a subject of the Austro-Hungarian Empire when World War I broke out, Malinowski was unable to travel freely in the Australian colony, but with his research well under way and turning necessity

Polish-born British anthropologist Bronislaw Malinowski is shown here during his fieldwork in the Trobriand Islands.

to advantage, he stayed on in the field, eventually accumulating two years of intensive experience. This kind of prolonged encounter in a single community was unique among ethnographers of the time and became a defining characteristic of British social anthropology in later years. His insistence that ethnographers try to see things "from the native's point of view" was also unusual for its time.

Malinowski showed that institutions such as law and complex economics, which many Westerners assumed to be the exclusive province of "civilized" societies, were possessed by "primitive" societies in full measure, if in a somewhat different form. In Malinowski's view primitive man was no "slave of custom" but a rational actor whose every practice and institution served a function that contributed to the satisfaction of individual and collective needs. Malinowski's approach, which came to be known as "functionalism," had wide-ranging influence throughout the social sciences. His deepest impact may have been made through the students he trained, particularly at the London School of Economics. They included many of the luminaries of classic British social anthropology: Raymond Firth, E. E. Evans-Pritchard, Isaac Schapera, Audrey Richards, Max Gluckman, and Jomo Kenyatta.

· · · · ·

The organized nature of social life became the principal focus of British social anthropologists between the 1920s and 1950s. Employing the concept of social structure—the idea that social relations are patterned and predictable—these anthropologists, led by Bronislaw Malinowski and A. R. Radcliffe-Brown, sought to understand the ways in which groups are formed in society, the rules governing the behavior of their members, how groups relate to one another, and the functions, both latent and manifest, that they perform. A classic example of this approach was Radcliffe-Brown's analysis of "joking" and "avoidance" relations. A "joking relationship" is one where one party "is permitted, and sometimes required to tease or make fun of the other, who in turn is required to take no offence." An example, drawn from Robert Lowie's account of the Crow Indians, might be the ribald behavior sanctioned between sisters- and brothers-in-law: a man "may treat his wife's sister with the utmost license, for example, raising her dress to expose her nakedness; and she may jest with him in corresponding fashion. One informant . . . was forever fondling and teasing his wife's younger sister, while she returned his treatment in kind. They were not in the least embarrassed by the wife's or my presence." Avoidance relationships, apparently the opposite of joking relationships, are characterized by extreme mutual respect and a limitation of direct personal contact. Older Navaho women traditionally wore tiny bells known as "mother-in-law bells" that were designed to warn sons-in-law of their approach so the men might absent themselves. Radcliffe-Brown asked himself what functions these seemingly bizarre (but widely found throughout the world) behaviors played in the societies in which they were performed.

The distinctive—and quite brilliant—analysis of Radcliffe-Brown was to look at "joking" and "avoidance" behavior as "standardized social

A. R. Radcliffe-Brown's analysis of the behavior of a Crow Indian man toward his wife's sister led him to believe that this pair's joking interactions constituted a standardized social relationship that provided them with a social script that allowed them to safely negotiate potentially awkward or disruptive relationships. This photograph of a group of Crow Indians in a teepee was taken in 1906 on the Crow Indian Reservation in Montana.

relationships" that represented not so much spontaneous ribaldry or shyness between two individuals, as a "structural situation" between a man and his mother-in-law or between two *categories* of people engaged in a difficult, delicate, and potentially disruptive social relationship. Looking at things in this way allowed Radcliffe-Brown to ask what the *function* of such "standardized social relationships" might be. He concluded that this sort of behavior was to be found primarily in "structural situations" in which the potential for conflict or social awkwardness is high—as between a man and his wife's mother or in the sexually charged relationship between a man and his wife's sister. Seen in this light, joking and avoidance were not opposites, but alternative ways of solving the same social problem: providing people with a kind of social script for getting around difficult "structural situations," either by allowing the most egregious behavior and requiring them not to take offence, or by prohibiting them from interacting at all.

· · · · ·

A. R. RADCLIFFE-BROWN (1881–1955)

A. R. Radcliffe-Brown was born in Birmingham and had a fairly conventional middle-class upbringing. He was educated at Cambridge, where he became a student of pioneering ethnologist W. H. R. Rivers and conducted research on the Andaman Islands in the Indian Ocean between 1906 and 1908. A few years later he participated in an expedition to Western Australia, where he concentrated on kinship and family organization. Radcliffe-Brown spent most of his academic career away from the UK, teaching at the universities of Cape Town, Sydney, and Chicago. He finally returned to Britain to take a position at Oxford in 1937.

British anthropologist A. R. Radcliffe Brown, who was primarily interested in social structure, or the formal rules governing the relationships within society, conducted research on the Andaman Islands in the Indian Ocean between 1906 and 1908. This illustration of Andaman Islanders building fishing boats is from the 1890s.

Radcliffe-Brown was profoundly influenced by the sociology of Émile Durkheim. Throughout his career he was primarily interested in social structure—the formal rules governing the relationships within society. His most brilliant work involved the analysis of structural "problems," such as the one concerning avoidance/joking relationships described in our text. He had little interest in—or patience for—Malinowski's concern with understanding the individual in society, and rejected Malinowski's drift toward seeing social institutions as ultimately concerned with filling biological needs. For Radcliffe-Brown society was a thing unto itself and his desire was to approach it as a natural scientist approaches any object of study. To distinguish himself from Malinowski he called his approach "structural functionalism" and looked at social anthropology as "comparative sociology" rather than a discipline with its own methods and research agenda.

· · · · ·

It is important to remember that the "functions" performed by a custom or an institution are not restricted to the "official" purpose assigned to them in the society's ideology. The "manifest" function of Peter's home institution, Williams College, is to provide young men and women with a sound education in the liberal arts. But the institution also provides these same young men and women with an opportunity to form social connections that will be economically valuable in their future lives and to find marriage partners who have similar characteristics of social and economic class, accomplishment, and values—a function borne out by the reputed high rate at which Williams alumni/ae marry each other. It is difficult, perhaps even impossible, to say to what extent this aspect of higher education in the

United States enters into the conscious decision-making processes of prospective students or even of their parents, but that the institution functions this way is hard to deny. As you can see, the idea of function, manifest and latent, is a powerful analytical tool. But it can also be an undisciplined one, since it is difficult to prove or disprove that a particular function is responsible for the character or durability of an institution or practice.

Radcliffe-Brown and other "structural functionalists" or "functionalists" used the idea of social structure to describe patterns of relations between individuals and groups and tended to explain those patterns in terms of their functions. For some, like Malinowski, these functions had to do with what he called a "doctrine of needs," that is, with supplying the basic wants of individual members of society, such as food, shelter, and so on. For others, these functions tended to be more concerned with the operation and perpetuation of institutions in society, a kind of overhead necessary for the maintenance of social relations. Eventually, because they saw social institutions as self-perpetuating in a state of "homeostatic equilibrium," a state in which all the parts acted to keep the whole in balance, the way a thermostat regulates heat in a house, and viewed social structure as constraining behavior, the functionalists were criticized for a vision of society that was essentially static and incapable of explaining social change. This was a particularly acute shortcoming given that many of the societies described by the functionalists had been colonized and were undergoing massive upheaval and reorganization. Today, we are more inclined to emphasize the dynamic properties of social life and the agency of individuals whose actions are both constrained and enabled by structure but have consequences—both intended and unintended—that can change structure.

French philosopher and anthropologist Claude Lévi-Strauss, whose *Elementary Structures of Kinship*, published in 1949, was regarded as one of the most important anthropological works on kinship, is shown here in a photograph taken in Paris in the 1980s.

Of course there are other important theorists who have proposed different views of the nature and origin of social structure. Claude Lévi-Strauss came to view social structures as existing to organize the flow of marriage partners among groups, seeing reciprocity, exchange, and alliance as defining social relations. For Lévi-Strauss, there was a significant difference between societies organized around various kinds of alliances between kin groups and societies in which marriage choices were "preferential." Lévi-Strauss was among those responsible for changing our thinking about society from that of an organic model to a cybernetic one. The parts of society were accordingly seen not so much as resembling organs in a body as constituting flows of data in a system of information. Naturally, too, the views of Karl Marx have given rise to an important school of anthropological thought. He regarded social life and the structure of society as contingent upon the dominant technologies of a given period and the ways people were organized to produce with these technologies.

More recently anthropologists seem to be less interested in the nature of social structure per se, shifting their attention to the ways in which power relations are perpetuated and contested in society. They view social structure as being as much a product of global economic and political forces as a product of purely local traditions. Nevertheless, in an important sense much of the fundamental intellectual apparatus of the functionalists remains in place: "Simple though it is," as Robert Murphy put it, "the idea that societies are systematized is central to the

Philosopher Karl Marx, who is shown here on a German stamp issued to commemorate the hundredth anniversary of his death, regarded social life and the structure of society as contingent upon the dominant technologies of a given period and the ways people were organized to produce with those technologies.

social sciences." Similarly, as Clifford Geertz and others have noted, virtually all explanations made by anthropologists of human behavior or human relations are couched in terms of the *functions* such behavior or relations perform.

Institutions

When patterns of behavior and ideology become relatively discrete, enduring, and autonomous, we call these patterns *institutions*. The most extreme form of institutions are those which Erving Goffman called "total institutions": the military, prisons, boarding schools, communes, cults, psychiatric hospitals, and so on. These are organizations that govern

What Canadian sociologist Erving Goffman's called total institutions—psychiatric hospitals, boarding schools, and the like—govern virtually all facets of their members' lives. This photograph shows Jack Nicholson and Danny DeVito performing in the Oscar-winning *One Flew Over the Cuckoo's Nest* (1975), directed by Milos Foreman.

virtually all facets of their members' lives. Individuals are typically stripped of previous social identities: their heads may be shaved, their clothes are replaced with uniforms, they lose access to many of their personal possessions, their everyday behavior is strictly regulated, and they are subject to the absolute authority of their immediate superiors. In this highly suggestive state they learn the institution's unique ways of doing, thinking, and feeling that may not necessarily be shared by the society at large. This experience is transformative, and years after leaving such an institution it continues to play a profound role in the individual's thoughts and feelings. The extreme degree of control and rigid patterning of behavior total institutions create often produces morally extreme results: from monastics living a life of holiness to the suffering inflicted upon the inmates of a concentration camp.

For more than a century social scientists and social philosophers have tended to make a sharp distinction between the institutions of "traditional" or "primitive" societies and those of "modern" societies. For example, Henry Maine, a nineteenth-century British lawyer, saw the shift from tradition to modernity as based on a shift from *status* to *contract*. In traditional society, he felt, people entered into relations with each other primarily on the basis of the social status they were assigned by birth, as in the social and economic relationship between a serf and his master. In modern society, however, social and economic relationships were subject, within limits, to negotiation between the parties concerned, such as between industrial workers and their employers. Other scholars stressed other contrasts. Ferdinand Tönnies made a distinction similar to Maine's between *Gemeinschaft* (community) and *Gesellschaft* (society). Lewis Henry Morgan pointed to the difference in an ideology of shared blood as a basis for forming society's main groups—as in American Indian societies formed of clans—and societies consisting of groups that stress residence in the same territory. Émile Durkheim felt that traditional societies were held together because all their members were basically alike (all hunters or farmers, all descended from a common ancestor, etc.), were largely self-sufficient, and therefore saw themselves in their compatriots. He called this "mechanical solidarity." Modern society, according to Durkheim, is characterized by the way its institutions create individuals who are divided into many different specializations, all of whom depend on each other. Thus in our society wheat farmers do not make their own bread from the wheat they grow, but buy it at the grocery store, depending on the efforts of millers, bakers, truckers, and a vast and complex array of other workers to put it there. Durkheim called this kind of arrangement "organic solidarity," seeing modern societies as composed of their parts the way an organism depends on the operation of separate but interdependent organs.

There have been many other attempts to use the characteristics of institutional relations to account for the difference between traditional and modern society. But the most influential of all such distinctions is Max Weber's idea of rationalization. Institutions are organized around the tasks they perform rather than on the social relations contained within them. In a way, Weber's notion of rationality is a marriage of structure and function. According to Weber, in "traditional" societies individuals participate in groups that perform multiple, overlapping roles and constitute social selves that pertain to all aspects of their lives, as, for example, the son of a chief is entitled to prerogatives on the basis of birth and throughout his social world. In contrast, a "modern" society typically has "rationalized institutions" in which it is a person's ability to perform specific tasks that counts more than other aspects of his or her social self. Moreover, the explicit rules and procedures that govern rationalized institutions derive

According to German sociologist and economist Max Weber (1864–1920), shown here in an undated photograph, in traditional societies individuals participate in groups that perform multiple, overlapping roles and constitute social selves that pertain to all aspects of their lives. In contrast, in modern societies, a person's ability to perform within rationalized institutions counts more than aspects of his or her social self.

their legitimacy not so much on an appeal to custom or tradition but from the logic and efficiency of the procedures themselves. In other words, modern institutions say, as it were, "We do not do things this way because we have always done things this way; we do things this way because it is the best way to get the job done.'

For Weber and many who have followed him, the quintessential modern institution is the bureaucracy. Although stereotyped as "rule by officials," Weber felt the key to understanding bureaucracy lay in the way it dealt with the modern problem of administration by organizing large groups of people in terms of impersonal goals and regulating the actions of its members through explicit sets of rules of procedure. Thus Weber identified such characteristics of the bureaucracy as the appointment and promotion of members based on contractual agreements, technical training, and experience as a formal condition of employment, fixed salaries, a strict separation of office and incumbent (the official does not own the means of administration), an ideology of meritocracy, and so on. We hear the voice of the bureaucrat in the reply "If it were up to me I'd be glad to help, but the rules won't let me."

Weber viewed the transition from traditional to modern institutions with considerable ambivalence. The traditional world, he felt, was a world of "enchantment," in which the individual felt spiritually integrated with the surrounding social and natural world. A move to rationality meant losing that feeling of spiritual integration. Weber's view of modern man was a dark one, of people imprisoned by their own rules and procedures in an "iron cage of rationality" from which there was no going back and no escape. Needless to say, Weber's characterizations need to be taken with a grain of salt. Weber realized, as anyone who has dealt with a government bureaucracy or a large corporation can tell you, that "rationalized institutions" often behave nonsensically and inefficiently, especially when rules are applied inflexibly. Similarly, the inhabitants of such organizations are often hired and promoted for reasons that have little to do with corporate efficiency, and they are far from immune to nepotism, corruption, or despotism. By the same token, traditional societies have been perfectly capable of organizing their affairs efficiently, and "enchantment" has a way of sneaking back into modern society where you least expect it: take for example, the popularity of New Age neopaganism in the postindustrial West.

The kinds of dichotomies that you can see in the table that distinguish between "traditional" and "modern" societies have often made anthropologists uncomfortable, and have done so for several reasons. These distinctions tend to be painted with a very broad brush indeed and easily lend themselves to stereotypes of non-Western societies, both negative and positive. It is easy—though hardly subtle—to think of non-Western people as irrational slaves of custom or, alternatively, as noble and mystical Friends of the Earth, when in fact they are something far more complex and far more interesting. Similarly, many of our dualistic expectations regarding the organization of "traditional societies" are, on closer examination, simply inaccurate. For example, John's host community in Santiago Nuyoo has governed itself for hundreds of years through something known more generally as the civil-religious hierarchy. This is an institution where virtually all adult men and women (usually as a married pair) serve in posts dedicated to civil and/or religious duties. Terms of office may last one to three years, and the offices are, as the name suggests, hierarchically arranged, so that people start out by serving in lower offices with lesser responsibilities and then as their experiences increase, "step high" as Nuyootecos say, to serve in offices with more responsibilities. The hierarchy is roughly pyramidal in shape, so that there are many offices at the bottom rank, and few at the top. Ideally this means that only men and women with the most experience (and wealth, since most positions are not salaried) can aspire to the highest offices and become respected elders or *tañuu* and *ñañuu*, "fathers" and "mothers of the community." In many respects, the features of the Nuyooteco civil-religious hierarchy, or "mountain of service," conform to Weber's characterization of a bureaucracy: there are explicit rules and procedures, an interlocking division of labor, an ideology of meritocracy, a separation of office and incumbent, and so on. Nuyootecos even speak in terms reminiscent of Weber's metaphor of an "iron cage," calling it "the punishment of community"—something necessary for collective life, but trapping and repressing them. Yet if Weber had been aware of them, he would have considered the "peasants" of Nuyoo a traditional society, specifically not given to bureaucratic forms of organization.

Have we begun to outgrow the iron cage of modernity? It is, of course, now fashionable to speak of "postmodernity," which has its own set of characteristics distinguishing it from modernity: modernity is positivist while postmodernity is relativist; modernity is based on industrial production while postmodernity is based on information flows; modernity generates knowledge through direct experience while postmodernity does so through simulation and modeling; modernity seeks holism while postmodernity celebrates pluralism; modernity is organized around the nation-state while postmodernity is found in transnational communities; and so on. We are as suspicious of these simplifying dualisms as we are of the dualisms used to distinguish "modern" from "traditional" society. But they have some utility. In anthropology postmodernism has concentrated primarily on a sharp critique of traditional methods of research and representation and has only just begun to produce a convincing vision of what postmodern social structures are like now or will be like in the future.

· · · · ·

TRADITION AND MODERNITY

Anthropologists and other social scientists have tended to view our own kind of society—complex, interdependent, large-scale, industrialized, in short modern—as a special case in the history of the world's societies. Many of them, particularly among the Victorians who stand at the origins of the social sciences, saw "traditional" societies in a sharp contrast with "modern" societies, and a series of distinctions have been used to characterize these differences. Here, in tabular form, are some of the most important of these contrasts, but we implore you, look upon them skeptically: they are often overly simplistic and sometimes just plain wrong-headed.

ANTHROPOLOGIST	TRADITIONAL SOCIETIES	MODERN SOCIETIES
Émile Durkheim (French, 1858–1917)	*Mechanical solidarity:* society is held together by the basic similarity of its members	*Organic solidarity:* society is held together by the interdependence of its parts and allegiance to common symbols
Ferdinand Tönnies (German, 1855–1936)	*Gemeinschaft* (community): traditional rules create a sense of universal solidarity among people	*Gesellschaft* (society): society is constituted by a deliberately formulated social contract which reflects rational self-interest
Lewis Henry Morgan (American, 1818–81)	*Common kinship* is the basis for collective identity	*Common territory* is the basis for collective identity
Sir Henry Maine (British, 1822–88)	*Status:* a person's rights and relationships are determined by the position in society assigned by birth	*Contract:* a person's rights and relationships are determined by negotiated but legally binding agreements with others
Max Weber (German, 1864–1920)	*Enchantment, tradition:* people relate to the world around them as participants in an animated whole; legitimacy is drawn from divine sources; positions and relations are determined by social status	*Rationality, modernity:* people see themselves as separate from the natural world; legitimacy derives from proven merit; institutions are organized for efficiency
Lucien Lévy-Bruhl (French, 1857–1939)	*Prelogical thinking:* the thought of "primitive" people is not illogical, but mystical and associative	*Logical thinking:* modern thought is dominated by logic and scientific method

$\bullet\ \ \bullet\ \ \bullet\ \ \bullet\ \ \bullet$

A Touch of Class: Social Reproduction

The fundamental institutions in any society exist beyond the lives of their individual members. They provide for continuity, as we saw in the case of "total institutions," through the active recruitment and socialization of new members. Yet this recruitment and socialization need not be as obvious as in the case of army recruits or college undergraduates, and is as much cultural as it is social. Recall, if you will, the sort of getting-to-know-you conversation we described at the beginning of this chapter. Such conversations, and especially the conversations of couples who are beginning to court but who do not yet know each other very well, often turn to a comparison of what we think of as "personal" tastes. What sort of music one likes, what sort of food, drink, clothing, and so on. What does this sort of knowledge tell us about someone else? Belonging to a social class is as much—maybe more—a matter of mastering an aesthetic repertoire as it is a matter of material wealth. Despite what the ancient Greeks may have said, we tend to find things beautiful because we have been taught to appreciate them and not because they are inherently beautiful. A taste for the subtleties of fine wines or abstract expressionist paintings is acquired as part of an elaborate and expensive education unavailable to most people. When we display our expertise in such matters we may sincerely appreciate what they represent, but we are also displaying that we have acquired connoisseurship, that we are members of an élite capable of appreciating "the finer things in life" and that we may be placed above those whose tastes run to cheap plonk and paintings of Elvis on velvet. The French anthropologist Pierre Bourdieu calls this "cultural capital." Combining the insights of Marx and Weber, Bourdieu views France, and the West in general, as divided into a number of specialized and relatively autonomous and hierarchically organized fields or institutions (such as the arts, sciences, law, business, and mass media) within which people are engaged in a constant struggle for position. In this struggle there are two major assets: financial capital and cultural capital, which are closely related. The competence to appreciate and consume things such as fine art or food is something that might begin in the home, with early childhood experiences. But that competence is also something that is purchased in the form of, for example, university training, which specializes in the knowledge needed to advance in given fields. This manifests itself on an individual level as a kind of second nature that distinguishes the individual from others who

Belonging to a social class is as much a matter of mastering an aesthetic repertoire as it is a matter of material wealth. A taste for abstract expressionist paintings places us above those whose tastes run to Elvis on velvet. This acquired connoisseurship is a form of cultural capital, according to French anthropologist Pierre Bourdieu, pictured here in a photograph from 1998.

have not enjoyed such training and background, so that class divisions are continuously reproduced in our own institutions. These boundaries are actively maintained in a variety of subtle ways.

Society and the Individual

Recall, if you will, the story of the Dou Donggo youth, la Ninde, that we told at the beginning of Chapter 1. He was accused and convicted of assaulting his aunt, ina Mone, but the case at heart had been about la Ninde's indiscreet courting of la Fia, who was betrothed to another young man. At one point when la Ninde was being admonished by the village elders for his behavior toward ina Mone and his indiscretions with la Fia, one of the elders said to him, "You think you belong to yourself, but you don't! You are owned by your parents, you are owned by your kinsfolk, you are owned by your village, you are owned by God. You can't just do as you please!'

When la Ninde was being reminded of the various people and groups who owned him, he was receiving a partial description of what anthropologists would call his "social identity." Each of us occupies a variety of positions in society and each of us has a set of rights and duties with respect to others occupying other, complementary positions. Each of us constitutes a unique set of social identities, but the number of identities and the rights and duties they entail are finite. Over the years this has remained a useful way of thinking about the individual and social relations.

La Ninde was also being reminded of one of the central contradictions of social life: we—especially those of us in modern, industrialized societies—tend to think of ourselves as autonomous individuals, possessed of the free will to make our own decisions even if we are, like la Ninde, constrained by the rules of society. After all, "society" is only an abstraction, isn't it, not a real living thing, but just a collection of individuals? Well, anthropologists, as have other social thinkers, swing back and forth between a vision of society as constituting what Durkheim called a "collective consciousness" and a view of social behavior that regards "society" as at most a statistical description of individual choices and actions. Certainly, in everyday talk we sometimes speak of "society" as if it were a living organism with a mind of its own, a whole that is greater than the sum of its parts. We blame "society" for just about every problem imaginable, from teenage pregnancy to personal feelings of depression. At the same time, if one were asked to point to where "society" is located, one would be no more able to do so than to be able to point to the dwelling place of God.

The problem is that each of us appears to be unique, unlike anyone else in the world, and the decisions we make are the product of unique and private mental processes. How many of us with children have remarked on their different dispositions? Yet at the same time, taken in the aggregate our decisions and their outcomes form clear and sometimes predictable patterns that correlate with other collective phenomena. Perhaps the most celebrated example of this paradox was discerned by Émile Durkheim in his extraordinary 1897 *Suicide*. The act of taking one's own life would seem to be the most personal and private of all possible decisions, each such decision purely unique. Yet Durkheim was able to show that in France, urban dwellers were more likely to commit suicide than those living in rural areas, and Protestants were more likely to commit suicide than Catholics or Jews. He argued that in the aggregate, rates of suicide corresponded to the degree to which individuals were integrated in their communities and the extent to which their communities provided them with a sense of worth and purpose. Individuals who were alienated from their social milieu were more likely to commit suicide, and some communities were more likely than others to alienate their members. At the same time, argued Durkheim, "altruistic" suicides resulted when individuals were so intensely committed to their social groups that negative social pressures in the form of shame or guilt or positive pressures promoting self-sacrifice to achieve a "higher" goal overcame instincts of self-preservation.

In the next chapter we will take a closer look at the kinds of groups and communities that make up societies. But before we do, we should point out that the theorists we have mentioned—Marx, Weber, Durkheim, and so on—are as likely to be found in an introduction to sociology as they are here. Erving Goffman, for example, who is widely identified as a sociologist, taught in the anthropology department that granted us our doctorates. He in turn dedicated one of his most important books to the memory of Radcliffe-Brown. The simple reason for this cross-fertilization and blurring of disciplinary boundaries is that the same broad moral and intellectual questions drive both anthropological and sociological research, questions such as the nature of collective life, the relations of the individual to the group, and, perhaps most importantly, how we are to understand our own time and collective dilemmas.

Nonetheless, anthropology and sociology retain distinct traditions and methods of research. Sociologists are much more likely to focus their research on urban, industrialized societies, and they tend to rely on the quantitative analysis of statistical data: the survey is perhaps their most important research tool. Consequently, sociologists are more likely to frame the results of their research as statements of social causality or correlation, such as linking drug use and homicide rates or unemployment and violent crime. Anthropologists continue to concentrate on exotic societies and to rely on participant observation as their chief method and are as concerned with sensitively portraying the texture of daily life as coming up with some universal proposition about social behavior. They are also much more inclined than sociologists to place their findings in the context of a cross-cultural comparison that includes many societies across time and space.

FOUR

Fernando Seeks a Wife:
Sex and Blood

●

THROUGHOUT THE HISTORY OF our species, perhaps even before we became fully human, our capacity for investing meaning in the world around us has been accompanied by a capacity for forming lasting bonds, emotional and practical, for the essential purposes of survival and procreation. We doubt anyone would dispute the idea that of the groups formed by those bonds the most fundamental are those formed on the basis of marriage and kinship. "Blood is thicker than water," goes the old proverb, and it is no accident that we have chosen the most elemental and life-sustaining of our bodily fluids as a metaphor for the ties of kinship.

One might think that the bases of ties of blood—marriage and the family—are both obvious and natural. As the American children's

The conventional Western view of the family, typified by this Philipp Friedrich von Hetsch (1758–1839) painting of Ferdinand Zeppelin and his family from 1808–9, is built around notions of romantic love between a man and a woman and their formation of a nuclear family household.

rhyme has it, "first comes love, then comes marriage, there they go with a baby carriage!" Our values and expectations about marriage and family are built around notions of romantic love between a man and a woman, their formation of a nuclear family household, jointly sharing all of life's joys, sorrows, and responsibilities. What anthropologists have discovered, however, is that marriage and the family may include all of these elements, some of them, none of them, or may be combined with other elements altogether.

Marriage, Family, and Household

Let's start with love and marriage. John was once walking down a path to visit a friend in Nuyoo whose wife had passed away two weeks before. He met the friend, Fernando, on the trail, ascending with a case of beer on his back. John asked the man where he was going, and Fernando told him he was going to make a marriage petition to the widowed daughter of a couple who lived not far from the center of town. John, who was more than mildly surprised that Fernando would be looking to marry again so soon after his wife's death, asked if he could come along. When they arrived at the house, Fernando set the case of beer down on the patio and proceeded to make a long, wandering speech, full of metaphor and poetic turns of phrase, asking for the woman's hand. The beer was distributed, and the woman's father launched into a speech of the same sort, telling Fernando no, but blaming his daughter for not having the qualities a fine man like Fernando would expect in a wife. After finishing the beer and taking their leave John and Fernando walked back together. Along the way John commented that it was "too bad things didn't work out," to which Fernando replied, "That's all right, I have another case of beer in the house, and I'm going to ask another woman tomorrow."

This incident taught John something important about Nuyooteco views of marriage. It was quickly apparent that romantic love played a very small role in Fernando's calculations. The woman who eventually married him had never even spoken to him before. What was foremost in Fernando's mind was the well-being of his children. In Nuyooteco reckoning it is nearly impossible for a man or a woman to maintain a household on his or her own. Any household that lacks a complement of adult male and female laborers is destined to fail. Indeed, in Mixtec, the word for widow(er), orphan, and indigent is the same. What Fernando was doing, so soon after his wife's death, was seeking out a partner who would perform the tasks that would complement his own, and thus ensure the continuity of his household. The women he approached (and he had to make three petitions before someone finally accepted) were each in a similar structural position: they were widows whose husbands had recently passed away.

John's story in turn reminds Peter of an instance he observed in Doro Ntika. A widow and a widower were about to join in a marriage that would unite their two half-households. A meeting was held to discuss the payment of a *co'i nika*, a brideprice, from the groom to the woman's parents and kin, which in the case of second marriages is usually a nominal one. To everyone's surprise, and despite much anguish and wailing on the widow's part, her dead husband's paternal kin announced their intention to assert their right to custody over the children of that union. Among the Dou Donggo, as among many peoples who observe the practice of paying a brideprice (or bridewealth as it is also called), the payment is felt not only to provide the bride's kin with compensation for the loss of her productive capacity, but also to secure the husband's kin's rights over the children of that marriage. In the case Peter observed, the status of the children was not changed by their father's death. His kin might not want his children—their kinsfolk—to come under the authority of another man if the mother remarried, and so they have the right to assume custody in the event she does. Usually this right is waived, but in this case they chose to exercise it. In practical terms, we might add, this would mean little: if the children did not continue to live with their mother, they would live right next door. But the point to be made here is that a marriage is often not merely the union of two individuals who form a new and independent social unit, as it is in

Marriage is often not simply the union of two individuals who form a new and independent social unit but an alliance between two groups of people, a union too important to be left to the principal actors. Russian painter V.V.Pukirev's *The Arranged Marriage* (1862) depicts the marriage of a young girl to an older man, probably for political or familial reasons.

our society. In many, perhaps most, of the world's societies a marriage is an alliance between two groups of people and is therefore too important to be decided by a pair of flighty teenagers. Moreover, a mother or father may not always have the first or best claim to the custody of his or her children, who may be seen as a precious resource by a larger collectivity of kin.

In both the Nuyoo and Dou Donggo examples we find that marriage is associated with transfers of wealth among the parties involved. These transfers serve to legitimate the marriage and acknowledge that a transfer of rights (in labor, in future children) has taken place between the different groups. Brideprice is a transfer of wealth from the male's group to the female's. Brideservice is a transfer of labor from the male's group to the female's. Dowry, something found in some European societies, does not so much transfer wealth from the woman's group to the man's (although it can end up that way) as it represents the woman's share of the inheritance children receive from their families. Although bridewealth payments often involve cash, frequently they are wealth items, which Mary Douglas has likened to "licenses" and "coupons" rather than money. On the one hand, the young man who wishes to marry is often dependent upon senior members of

Waiting for the groom. Dou Donggo women sit on the doorway of a house waiting for someone to bring an installment of a *co'i nika*, or brideprice, as the first stage in a wedding. The fiancé's family is late, which is why they look so anxious. In the end, the bridegroom's family postponed the wedding and tried to renegotiate the sum of the brideprice. Eventually they married.

his kin group to provide the items needed to make the payment. These senior members of the group are willing to give up these valuables because he has shown he is responsible and loyal, thus in effect licensing him to make the step into adulthood. On the other hand, the wealth items used for bridewealth payments cannot or should not be used in just any transaction. In Mary Douglas' example—the use of raffia cloth for bridewealth by the Lele of Zimbabwe—she found that no one would go into the marketplace and exchange the cloth for something like food or sell it for money. It was far too valuable for that, since raffia was used for things money can't buy—brides. Bridewealth items can thus function like coupons in that they can be redeemed only for certain things and in certain ways. Moreover, in many societies, the only way a group can acquire the "coupons" it needs to obtain spouses for its members is by marrying off its women to other groups and receiving them as bridewealth payments, thereby locking all the groups into a series of marriage exchanges.

Marriage in many cultures is associated with transfers of wealth among the parties involved. This 1840 Indian marriage certificate obliges Bahadur Shah II, who was the last Mughal ruler in India, to pay one-third of the brideprice immediately upon his marriage to the bride, Begum Zeenat Mahal, and two-thirds at sometime during their married life.

This perspective aids in understanding practices such as the levirate (a man marries his brother's childless widow) and the sororate (a woman marries her sister's widower), both typically encountered in patriarchal societies. Perhaps the earliest recorded instance of a levirate marriage comes in the Hebrew Bible (Genesis 38:8–10). Judah's firstborn dies without issue and so he orders his second son, Onan, to "go in to your brother's wife and marry her, and raise up an heir to your brother." Onan knew that any child of this marriage would technically be his dead brother's, and would inherit from Judah's patrimony instead of Onan and his own sons. So it was "when he went in to his brother's wife, that he spilled his seed on the ground, lest he should given an heir to his brother. And the thing which he did displeased the Lord; therefore he killed him also." Despite what generations of Sunday-school teachers may have claimed, Onan's sin was not one of self-indulgence, nor did hair grow upon his palms. His sin was his refusal to facilitate the continuation of his dead brother's (patrilineal) line. In the case of sororate marriage, the idea seems to be one of fulfilling a contractual obligation on the part of a dead woman's kin to provide her husband with a wife. In both cases— and this seems to be the central point—the marriage relationship is one contracted between two groups of kin and persists beyond the lives of those actually married. Moreover, an interest in the continuation of the deceased's line rests at the heart of these obligations.

If, as in the case of the levirate, marriage does not require that both partners be living, neither need it require that partners be of the opposite sex. E. E. Evans-Pritchard, who worked in the Azande kingdoms of central Africa in the 1930s, reported that warriors would sometimes marry young boys, who would perform wifely duties, including those of a sexual nature. Such marriages included paying a brideprice to the boy's family, and if someone else had sexual relations with the boy the warrior could bring charges of adultery. Similarly, in ancient Dahomey (now Benin) a wealthy woman might marry a younger woman who was expected to take male lovers so as to produce heirs. In each of these cases the conventions, rights, and obligations surrounding marriages between men and women also apply. While these examples seem akin to the same-sex marriages some advocate in the West, it should be pointed out that the Azande and Dahomey same-sex marriages, as well as others reported in the ethnographic literature, are based on explicit asymmetries, not the kind of partnership and equality that Western advocates of same-sex marriages have in mind.

The Dou Donggo, like many Southeast Asian peoples, approach relations between the genders as based on a deep and abiding complementarity that extends beyond household decisions to include deeper spiritual matters. The unit of village citizenship is the married couple. Couples engage in rituals as couples, and a whole series of initiation rituals that occur during the life cycle of a couple can be officiated over only by ritual specialists who are married themselves and whose spouses are still alive.

For the Dou Donggo the expectation of a lifetime bond with a single partner is well established. In many societies, however, neither assumption holds. *Polygyny*, whereby a man has more than one wife, is common. Islamic law permits a man to have as many as four wives—although most Muslims are monogamous—so long as he is able to provide for them and treats them equally. In many instances of polygyny, especially in Africa, each wife has a separate household, which the husband visits serially. *Polyandry*, whereby a woman has more than one husband, is far less common, and is best known from Tibet and the hills of northern India. Tibetan polyandry, at least, is not the mirror image of polygyny, but usually entails the joint marriage of a group of brothers to one woman. The demographic consequences of polyandry are just the opposite of polygyny: since a woman normally gives birth only every few years, and usually to only one child at a time, a polyandrous marriage tends to slow population growth and conserve heritable resources such as land. Polygyny, on the other hand, contributes to population growth and the rapid dissipation of land resources among heirs. Monogamy, polygyny, and polyandry are far from mutually exclusive, but may show up in a given society in response to economic and ecological circumstances. An expectation that marriage will be a lifelong bond is also highly variable, as has been witnessed in our own society in recent generations, when divorce has gone from something rare and shameful to something commonplace and morally neutral.

Expectations of the marriage bond vary widely among cultures. Although it has changed with the societal normalization of divorce, the typical Western marriage was viewed as a lifetime bond with a single partner. In other societies, polygyny (marriage of one man to more than one wife) and polyandry (marriage of one woman to more than one man) are common. This late-nineteenth-century engraving shows a Central African man and his wives.

Given all the variations in forms, practices, and values associated with marriage, in what sense can we talk about it as a universal human institution? Is there such a thing as "marriage" or have we simply lumped a mishmash of different customs and practices together and given it the name of the social institution we are most reminded of? This kind of question is a genuine problem for anthropology. Intuitively we look at these divergent practices and values and something tells us there is a common thread, but when we try to formulate a unitary definition that covers all known cases, things begin to fall apart. One way of approaching the problem is to set aside a concern for what it is that marriage *is* and ask ourselves what problems are there in human experience that marriage attempts to solve. Ward Goodenough defined marriage as "a transaction and resulting contract in which a person (male or female, corporate or individual, in person or by proxy) establishes a continuing claim to the right of sexual access to a woman . . . and in which the woman involved is eligible to bear children." What problems would an institution that fits this description solve? To begin with, it would seem that marriage has to do with regulating sex. Other species of primates either live in large social groups, in which case access to sexually receptive females is governed by a pecking order among the males (chimpanzees or baboons), or live as isolated "domestic" groups, which are either "monogamous" pair-bonds (orangutans) or cases in which dominant males enjoy exclusive access to a "harem" of females (gorillas). Only humans are both social *and* pair-bonding, and only among humans are adult females sexually receptive all the time (at least in theory). This is a situation with tremendous potential for conflict and confusion and it seems only likely that humans should seek to use their capacity for cultural behavior to impose some sort of order on the whole business. While, if truth be admitted, the potential

While other primates, for example, baboons (pecking-order access to females), orangutans (monogamous pair bonds), and gorillas (dominant male with a harem), are organized in ways that regulate sex, human social organization creates tremendous potential for conflict and confusion. This photograph, taken in 1981, shows a silverback gorilla in Rwanda, Africa, moving his group forward.

for conflict and confusion may not have been eliminated, that there is so much variation in the solutions humans have developed is a tribute to the very cultural nature of marriage. Similarly, social reproduction begins with sexual reproduction. Some means of both assigning responsibility for and expressing an interest in the next, dependent, generation is also accommodated by the various ideas and practices we call "marriage."

While the nuclear family—a married couple and their children—might be held up as the natural and most basic family unit by some Western social scientists, our discussion of the complexities and variation to be found in marriage should hint that the family is the subject of tremendous variation in human experience. Anthropologists have learned that societies get along quite well with family units that are both more extensive and less extensive than the nuclear family. A family can be as minimal as a mother and her children or as elaborate as an Indian joint fraternal family in which parents live with their unmarried children, their married sons, and the wives and children of those sons. The dynamics between the mother-in-law and her daughters-in-law and among the daughters-in-law who compete for recognition is the subject of many an Indian domestic drama. And in yet another model for domestic arrangements, there are societies in both the Amazon basin and highland New Guinea where men and adolescent boys live together collectively in a men's house while women, their daughters, and their young sons live in separate households. Their husbands and fathers visit them from time to time, but rarely spend the night.

A single society may easily accommodate a variety of family types. Similarly, we must not regard these domestic units as static, but rather as

The family is the subject of tremendous variation in human experience. In some societies in the Amazon basin and highland New Guinea, men and adolescent boys live collectively in a men's house, while women and their daughters and young sons live in separate households. This late-twentieth-century photograph shows paintings covering the walls of the men's house of a highland tribe in Papua New Guinea.

being subject to a complex developmental cycle. Among the Dou Donggo, traditionally, a marriage might begin before the bride and groom are even born. Good friends might pledge to betroth their children if, of course, they are of opposite sex. However a betrothal was begun, if two young people were to be married a brideprice would be negotiated and partially paid at the time of the wedding. The newlyweds would typically live in the house of the bride's parents for a year or two while the groom provided brideservice to his father-in-law in exchange for their keep. The Dou Donggo say that the motive for this arrangement was to allow a young woman to be in comfortable and familiar surroundings with her mother when her first child was born. After the birth of the first child, the marriage would enter a new stage: the groom's family would pay the remainder of the brideprice and the couple would move into a house of their own, usually near the family of the groom. There they would raise their own children, eventually taking in sons-in-law as had been the case for them earlier. In old age a couple might move to a smaller house in their gardens, where a steady stream of grandchildren would be detailed to live with them, keeping them company and helping with domestic tasks. A widow or widower might continue to live alone with help from grandchildren, or might move in with an adult child, usually a daughter. In recent years this pattern has shifted a bit, to one in which the stage of brideservice and residence in the bride's family's house is omitted and the couple move into their own house immediately on marriage. Their house is usually built near to that of the bride's family (so she will be near her mother when she bears her first child), so ultimately a village compound is created consisting of a group of sisters and their households. If you were to look at many Dou Donggo households you would see what looks like a "nuclear family" resembling our own Western model. But it would be quite misleading to see it that way, since the "nuclear family" is but a part of a wider picture. Similarly, child rearing, which is one of the central undertakings of the family, is virtually never surrendered to a child's parents alone, but is shared by grandparents, aunts and uncles, and others who happen to be nearby. Children move about from house to house, eating where they are hungry and sleeping where they happen to be when darkness falls. Indeed, in practical terms the nuclear family is a very inefficient child-rearing unit, poorly suited to the task.

Finally, there is an important sense in which families need to be seen as units in larger processes of alliance, as pieces of a political chess game. Claude Lévi-Strauss argued that in idealized terms the minimal unit of kinship includes the wife's brother, representing the family that has "given" her to her husband. Lévi-Strauss is convinced that the most "elementary" form of marriage is one in which two men exchange sisters and the offspring of the two marriages renew the alliance by marrying their cousins. This may sound mildly scandalous or even incestuous to us, but in fact there are a number of societies in which marriage to a cousin is not merely permitted or desirable but practically obligatory. When men marry their mothers' brothers' daughters for several generations in succession a marriage alliance is formed between two lines of male descendants. When men marry their father's brother's daughters in successive generations (a pattern much favored in the Middle East) a line of descent through males is kept strong; if this is a pastoral society it will be easier to keep the group's flocks together.

My Milk, My Blood: Kinship and Descent

The command by Judah to Onan to marry his sister-in-law so as to sire an heir for his dead brother shows that the relationship between the biological facts of paternity (or maternity) and the social ideology of parentage is a complex and culturally arbitrary one. Anthropologists have discovered that while no society ignores the role of biology in procreation, all societies to some extent imagine the facts of sex differently and may use those imagined facts as much metaphorically as literally. In Nuyoo, for example, people recognize the possibility of *partible* maternity and paternity, that is, that an individual can have more than one "biological" father or mother. Partible maternity occurs when an individual is born of one mother, and then breastfed by another. In Nuyooteco thinking, children and parents are linked by their sharing of blood. This link is established in the womb when the baby receives its mother's blood through the umbilical cord. Once the baby is born, it continues to receive its mother's blood, in the form of breast milk. This is why mothers will refer to children as "my milk, my blood." It sometimes happens that a mother dies soon after birth or is otherwise unable to breastfeed. The family will then call in a wet nurse who will give her breast milk to the child. This second woman then becomes linked to the child by a blood tie and the child will grow up also referring to this woman as mother.

Partible paternity, on the other hand, begins with the idea most Nuyootecos have that to become pregnant a woman has to have sex numerous (some say at least ten) times. The reason for this is that she needs to accumulate a critical mass of semen (the "white blood" of males which in some Mixtec dialects is the same word as milk) in her womb, out of which a fetus will begin to grow. Partible paternity occurs when she has sex with more than one man while accumulating the necessary mass of semen to become pregnant. Not surprisingly, people do not publicly acknowledge partible paternity with the same enthusiasm as they do partible maternity (however, it may have consequences for inheritance and marriage).

Throughout the world the idea that individuals who share blood (or milk, bone, or whatever substance is felt to be transmitted in procreative acts) are bound to one another by powerful ties is the basis for domestic and child-rearing groups. But it can also be a basis for much larger social, political, and economic entities. In many societies, especially those of Africa, an ideology of shared descent was the principal way societies were organized. A lineage is a group of people formed by their descent from a known common ancestor. Clans, in turn, are groups of lineages whose members recognize descent from a common ancestor, although the precise calculation of these links may not be possible, and the ancestor may be a mythical being, special object, or animal totem. Anthropologists have learned that there are several ways that people may reckon descent, which have different and significant social consequences.

For patrilineal groups, descent is reckoned in the male line. A patrilineage, then, consists of those people, male and female, to whom I am related because we are all descended from a common ancestor through exclusively male father–child links. If one thinks of the way surnames have been traditionally transmitted in the English-speaking world, one can get a good idea of how membership in a patrilineage is reckoned. Since it is, after all, "a wise child who knows his own father," societies built around patrilineal descent are often also patriarchal and show a kind of institutional anxiety over unlicensed sexual access to women. Virginity in women before marriage and sexual fidelity by women after marriage may be

There are several ways that people can determine descent, which have different and significant social consequences. Clans, for example, are groups of lineages whose members recognize descent from a common ancestor, which may be a mythical being, special object, or animal totem. This ancestor figure of the Bakor people, from Basalt, Nigeria, was created sometime before the sixteenth century.

highly prized and stringently enforced, leading to practices such as purdah (the seclusion of women) and veiling.

For matrilineal groups, descent is reckoned in the female line. Just as women do not transmit the affiliation of their birth to their children in a patrilineage, men do not transmit their affiliation to their children in a matrilineage. Societies that are built around matrilineal descent, however, are not necessarily matriarchal. Indeed, although the political status of women may be better in a matrilineal society than in a patrilineal one, men still tend to dominate political and public affairs in matrilineal societies. But because of the nature of matrilineal descent, a man's principal heir is not his son, but his sister's son and, conversely, a man looks not to his father or his father's brothers for guidance and support, but to his mother's brothers and their mother's brothers, who are his clanmates. Although the theory remains

Societies built around patrilineal descent are often patriarchal and can show a kind of institutional anxiety over unlicensed sexual access to women, leading in some cases to practices such as purdah, in which a woman must cover her body and conceal her form, as shown in this early-twentieth-century photograph of a woman in purdah from Sarmarkand, Uzbekistan.

controversial, Bronislaw Malinowski, who did his principal fieldwork among the matrilineal Trobriand Islanders, suggested that in matrilineal societies the anxieties of the Oedipus complex are directed not at a maturing boy's father, but at his mother's brother. Malinowski felt that the principle behind the complex had to do with a conflict toward male authority in a context of emerging adolescent sexuality, and since the authority figure in a matrilineage is a boy's mother's brother rather than his father, it would be directed there.

There are other modes of descent, such as double unilineal descent, in which different kinds of group membership are transmitted according to matrilineal and patrilineal principles, so that everyone is simultaneously a member of at least two distinct descent groups. There are also societies in which important groups are formed on the basis of "non-unilineal" descent. This is a reckoning of descent through a combination of male and female links back to an important ancestor. For example, a political dynasty such as the Kennedys in the United States includes Shrivers, Smiths, and even Schwarzeneggers, but all of them are—or are married to—descendants of Joseph Kennedy.

Finally, many societies, notably our own, do not usually form kin-groups on the basis of descent from a common ancestor, but rely on being able to trace ties of blood to a common relative, usually a living one. Although having a relative in common, the members of a kindred, as these groups are called, need not be related to one another. We typically include cousins in our kindreds, but the children of our mother's brother are not related to the children of our father's brother. Moreover, membership in kindreds tends to depend more on keeping up active social relations than on anything else. A cousin who is geographically distant may fade from the kindred more quickly than one who is genealogically distant but nearby.

In non-unilineal descent, a reckoning of descent is made through a combination of male and female links back to an important ancestor, such as Joseph Kennedy, in the case of the Kennedy political dynasty in the United States. This 1986 photograph of Maria Shriver and Arnold Schwarzenegger's wedding party shows descendants of Joseph Kennedy through both male and female links, including his sons Robert and John and his daughters Eunice and Patricia.

Throughout the greater part of human history, and even in many places today, groups formed on the basis of kinship and descent have been the principal means for owning property and regulating the lives of their members. It is important to remember that while the principles upon which such groups are formed may be fairly clear-cut, in actual practice lineages, clans, and kindreds acquire and discharge members in all kinds of ways that may have little to do with the official ideology of descent or kinship. Adoption, fosterage, ritual, and even bondage are all means by which members may be recruited to a kin group. These and other examples have made it abundantly clear to anthropologists that in analyzing kin groups we should keep in mind the complex relationships that may exist among the biological, the social, and the cultural (or ideological) when humans are creating and maintaining relationships with one another.

FIVE

La Bose Becomes Bakar: Caste, Class, Tribe, Nation

•

NOT ONLY IS BLOOD THICKER than water; it also makes a pretty good social glue. So the glue that holds families and clans together, although not perfect, at least has the virtue of undeniable ideological power. Many simpler societies are made up almost exclusively of groups that take kinship, marriage, and descent as the rationale for their formation, operation, and perpetuation. But what about more complex societies, such as our own? We have created a great many different kinds of groups, ranging from hobby clubs to religious congregations to the nation-state and beyond. Some very large groups like castes, ethnic groups, and even nations continue to rely on an ideology of shared blood, even when genealogical

While it seems reasonable to take as the basis of solidarity in a primitive society the homogeneity of its members, what becomes problematic is how to create differences. Totemic identifications—with animals, plants, or natural phenomena—are ways of distinguishing peoples who are otherwise indistinguishable from one another. This photograph of a young girl seated in front of two totem poles was taken in Alaska around 1895.

links cannot be traced. In contrast, the common interests that hold groups like hobby clubs or labor unions together is altogether different from the ideology that unites a caste or an ethnic group.

At the end of the nineteenth century Émile Durkheim looked at his own society and saw a France demoralized by a humiliating defeat at the hands of Prussia, beset with the dislocations of urbanization and industrialization, and challenged in its institutions of order and authority by increasingly well-organized and militant working-class political movements. To Durkheim the ability of the French nation to endure seemed very much in doubt and the question, "what holds society together?" seemed to be the most pressing problem facing modern Western society. In our time, too, race riots, ethnic fratricide, and revolutions, from Watts, Brixton, Bosnia, Rwanda, to the killing fields of

Cambodia make us wonder if *any* society can hold together indefinitely. Durkheim, as mentioned in Chapter 3, approached this problem by looking at *The Division of Labour in Society* and by making a distinction between simpler societies, in which there is little occupational specialization and members very much resemble one another, and more complex societies,

Émile Durkheim's investigation into what holds society together was spurred by France's humiliating defeat in the Franco-Prussian War, the dislocations inherent in urbanization and industrialization, and the challenges the country faced in its institutions of order and authority. This hand-colored lithograph from 1870 or 1871 shows the Sisters of Mercy arriving on the battlefield to succor the wounded after the Battle of Gravelotte, the largest battle of the war.

in which individuals and groups each specialize in a particular kind of productive activity, their other needs being met by the output of other individuals and groups—modern, industrial societies being the ultimate example of the latter. He called the social glue holding simpler societies together "mechanical solidarity," while he characterized more complex societies as held together by "organic solidarity" because they operated like biological *organisms*, with each organ of the body having its specialized function but supported by all the other organs.

The questions Durkheim raised about the nature of solidarity continue to inform anthropological research, although things turn out to be considerably more complex than we intuitively suspect. Let us take the idea that the basis of solidarity in a so-called primitive society is the homogeneity of its members. While on its face this seems reasonable, experience indicates that in some places it is precisely the social sameness of human beings that constitutes the pressing social problem people face. In societies where homogeneity is a given, what becomes problematic is how to create differences—even differences that seem as basic to us as those between males and females. Take, for example, totemic clans—kin groups named after animals, plants, or natural phenomena (thunder, lightning, and in one rather unsettling case from Australia, a puddle of dog vomit)—which are remarkably widespread in the world. Such identifications provide a means for people who are otherwise indistinguishable from one another except for accidents of birth, to declare, in effect, "my group is as different from other groups as one species of animals is from another." This kind of difference for the sake of difference transfers into the modern world as well: in the United States, colleges and universities that are in the larger scheme of things indistinguishable from one another strike up fierce rivalries among themselves, adopting distinctive emblems and colors and naming their sports teams in much the same way as totems are named. Thus Peter's home institution, Williams College, is a small, New England liberal arts school very much like its rival, Amherst College; yet students at the two schools revel in adopting attitudes that magnify incidental differences between the two, and playfully characterize each other as personifications of evil on earth. What does this accomplish? In part it enhances feelings of belonging and it also provides a multitude of opportunities—athletic contests prominent among them—for students and alumni/ae to participate in an enthusiastic ritual expression of solidarity. Durkheim called this kind of experience "collective effervescence." He identified it as the root of the religious experience, as well as placing it at the heart of social solidarity.

At the same time, a large, complex society that epitomizes Durkheim's organic solidarity, where the basis of solidarity is the complex interdependence of its many distinct parts, may be intently concerned with constructing a vision of itself as a homogeneous entity. This process is particularly evident in the new states that emerged after the dissolution of colonial empires in the last century. With varying degrees of success, national languages were ratified, a common history was taught in the schools, and a set of patriotic figures and symbols, derived from the shared past, were made to stand for the new nation. Symbols of the nation—flags, anthems, public monuments, and the like—and elaborate civic rituals accompanied by a national mythology that legitimized the nation-state were created and displayed as a means of providing a common national consciousness. Durkheim called these "collective representations," recognizing the symbolic nature of social solidarity. It seems ironic in the extreme that simple, homogeneous societies are intent on creating difference where little exists, while complex, heterogeneous societies must strain mightily to create unity out of organic diversity.

Identity and "Shared Blood"

In the last chapter we looked at some of the ways in which cultures interpret—or ignore—the facts of procreation in ideologies of kinship. Similar ideologies are often used to create feelings of unity and shared destiny in larger groups, whose members may have no traceable genealogical connection. Among the most interesting of these is the Hindu caste system. Classic Hindu cosmology provides a coherent model of a fixed social order that combines marriage within the group (and therefore shared blood), occupational specialization (and therefore the division of labor in society), and relative degrees of spiritual purity (and therefore hierarchical ranking). In theory every person is born into a *jati*, a group which has a local monopoly on a particular occupation (such as blacksmiths, weavers, and so on). A person takes a spouse from within the *jati*, as do all of the person's descendants. The various *jatis* are hierarchically ranked with respect to one another, a ranking that is reinforced in daily behavior by prohibitions against higher-caste individuals taking food or drink from those of a lower caste. All of this is supported by an elaborate system of meaning and belief, much of it given spectacular ritual expression, that lies at the heart of Hinduism. In reality, of course, things are more fluid and complex, especially in contemporary India: *jatis* are actually far from endogamous, individuals are free to pursue occupations not reserved to a specific *jati* in a particular place, and the relative rankings of *jatis* turn out to shift over time and space in subtle ways.

The Hindu caste system is one way a larger group created feelings of unity and shared destiny among members who have no traceable genealogical connection. This photograph of a school of untouchables was taken near Bangalore in 1935.

Ideologies of ethnicity also base collective identity on shared descent, usually relating to a common regional or national origin. Language, dress, occupational specialization, and religion, among other things, may also be a part of an ethnic identity. Since ethnic groups are always defined vis-à-vis other ethnic groups, the mere fact of difference is what is often more important than anything else. Thus the specific content of ethnic identities may shift wildly with time, and what may really be at stake is not any profound differences in culture or worldview, but how a particular ethnic group membership allows access to scarce resources or how it can be used by leaders to further their political goals. Consequently, we see that an ethnic affiliation is often one of a series of group memberships

The last *ncuhi*. This picture of la Honte was taken a few years before his death. He was the last *ncuhi*, or "high priest," in the traditional religion of the Dou Donggo. The ethnic separateness of the Dou Donggo had long depended on their traditional religion and a special relationship with the sultan of Bima. By the time la Honte died in 1983 most Dou Donggo were Muslims or Christians and there was no longer a sultan ruling in Bima, so it was felt there was little reason to replace the last *ncuhi*.

individuals maintain, which are contextually activated, often in response to strategic interests. One problem with a term like "ethnicity" is that it is used to refer to groups in all sorts of different situations, so its conceptual usefulness is reduced. It is clear, however, that the political mobilization of people based on an ethnic identity remains a dynamic and often highly destructive force throughout the modern world, a force that shows little sign of abating. Since ethnic groups are frequently defined vis-à-vis one another in moral terms, ethnic conflicts, whatever may ultimately have ignited them, can be vicious, with contending parties opposing one another as "good" versus "evil."

Another story from Peter's experiences among the Dou Donggo may serve to illustrate how some of these characteristics of ethnicity play out in real life.

The Dou Donggo live adjacent to the much more numerous lowland Bimanese. The Bimanese converted to Islam early in the seventeenth century, but the Dou Donggo by and large refused to join them and remained true to their traditional beliefs. In the past three decades most of the Dou Donggo have become either Muslim or Christian with varying conviction, but the lowland Bimanese continue to regard them with the suspicion and contempt reserved for infidels. In this way, and others, differences of culture, language, and belief emerged between the lowland Bimanese and highland Dou Donggo that I would regard as constituting an "ethnic boundary." The couple who lived two houses away from me in the village of Doro Ntika were named ama Bose and ina Bose. (The Dou Donggo follow a practice called "teknonymy" whereby after the birth of their first child parents are addressed as "Father of" or "Mother of" that child. So when Bose was born his father came to be called "ama Bose" and his mother "ina Bose.") Ama Bose had converted to Islam a few years ago but his son still bore a traditional Dou Donggo name. A year or so before the time came for young Bose to be sent away to school in the lowlands his father announced to me and everyone else that henceforth Bose would be known as Bakar (a good Muslim name) and that he would be called ama Bakar. He was quite open about the fact that he had decided this was necessary in order for his son to have a better chance at succeeding in the Bimanese school he would attend. "If he continues to be called Bose," my neighbor said, "his schoolmates will make fun of him and his teachers will be cruel to him." Most of the people in the village acquiesced in the name change, and started calling the boy "Bakar," but most of us also continued to call his father "ama Bose."

It is not unusual for someone to disguise their origins in contexts where that identity is a liability, and being non-Muslim in Indonesia can be a distinct liability. But a more subtle process may also be at work. For one thing, we can see that "ethnic boundaries" are often a good deal more permeable than they seem to be; people may move back and forth across them with a surprising degree of ease. For another, ethnic boundaries are less permanent than they often appear. As the differences of religion, custom, and language that created the distinction between Dou Donggo

Ama Bose with his son, Bose, who is holding his little sister, la Asani. Bose is a traditional Dou Donggo name. In Bima people are called after their children once they have them, so Bose's father is called ama Bose, or "Father of Bose." A year or so before young Bose was to be sent away to school in the rigorously Muslim lowlands, his father announced that Bose would henceforth be known as Bakar, a common Muslim name, and that he would be called ama Bakar.

and Bimanese begin to disappear, it seems likely that the boundary may be substantially renegotiated, if not disappear altogether. And of course to most Indonesians outside the local context of Bimanese–Dou Donggo ethnicity, the two are indistinguishable. The very malleability and permeability of the form and content of ethnic distinctions are what make ethnicity both endlessly fascinating and conceptually slippery.

· · · · ·

NATIVE AMERICANS IN THE UNITED STATES

In 1960 the National Census Bureau in the United States began to use self-identification to ascertain an individual's race and ethnicity. In the thirty-year period between 1960 and 1990 the number of people identifying themselves as Amerindians grew from 524,000 to 1,878,000—a growth rate far exceeding anything that could be attributed to natural increase alone. It appears that at least half of this increase, perhaps more, was due to people changing their ethnic identifications. The reason for this has much to do with government policies that have accorded legal status to Native Americans and the material advantages such descent might confer. Tribal businesses for some groups are thriving, government transfer payments are often earmarked for the members of tribal groups, and private foundations specifically target Native Americans for support and services. Some Native American groups have had to adopt strict criteria for tribal affiliation so they will not be swamped by new members. But a great deal of the rise in the numbers of people identifying themselves as Native Americans has to do with the way personal identities are tied up with larger public narratives. In sharp contrast to the situation forty years ago, when Amerindians were almost inevitably depicted in film, television, and in popular print as bloodthirsty savages, they are now portrayed in a

A great deal of the dramatic growth of the population of Native Americans has to do with how personal identities are tied up with larger public narratives. Whereas Native Americans are now portrayed in a sympathetic, even romantic light, in the past they have been portrayed in film, television, and popular print as bloodthirsty savages, as, for example, in this illustration of a Modoc Indian, from southern Oregon, holding up the scalp of a dead soldier, published in the May 17, 1873, issue of *Harpers Weekly*.

sympathetic, even romantic light. With over seven million people today in the United States reporting some degree of Native American ancestry, the numbers of Native Americans in future censuses will most likely continue to increase at a very high rate.

· · · · ·

While categories of caste and ethnicity are often used to rank the members of a society and limit or ease their chances in life, *race* goes much further by dividing the entire human species into a limited number of categories that are ideologically associated with variable degrees of intelligence, beauty, capacity for ethical behavior, and other characteristics. This idea of race is particularly powerful in reinforcing inequality because it is naturalized, unquestioned, and frequently accepted even by the victims of racism. Specific national and regional manifestations of racism often seem to reproduce the global hierarchy of races. Thus Mixtec speakers will rank themselves above African-Mexican populations on the Pacific coast of Oaxaca and Guerrero in terms of a range of personal qualities, but below European populations with regard to these same qualities. As we noted in Chapter 2, one of the intellectual projects of the Boasian anthropologists was to show that the physical distinctions upon which racial types are based do not hold, since physiological traits so overlapped that it was impossible to define discrete human types. And they were at pains to show that racialist explanations for human differences are unable to substantiate the links between physical form and things such as language, culture, and intelligence. We are reminded of the case of a rural village in Brazil, whose inhabitants are descendants of Africans, Europeans, Amerindians, Middle Eastern populations, and even Asians. According to our colleague Catherine Howard, people there feel that a family can produce children of all different colors, so that it is not unusual for a couple to have a black child, a white child, and a brown child just as some of their children will be tall while others short.

What distinguishes race from ethnicity? Both categories are what we could call "culturally constructed" categories: they have some relationship—often erroneous—to facts of biology, but are primarily social categories designed to characterize oneself and others, often with moral overtones. Ethnicity tends to emphasize matters of culture, language, and religion: part of the legal definition of "Malay"

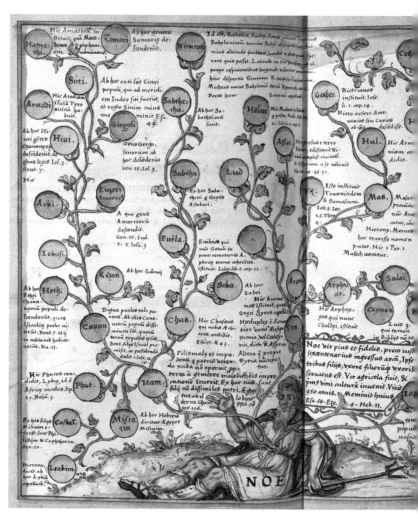

The culturally constructed category of race emphasizes easily recognized physical characteristics and tends to rely on a folk theory of biological origins, sometimes with a mythological base, such as the idea that the races of the world originated with the sons of Noah, as depicted, for example, in this sixteenth-century vellum from the *Biblia sacrosancta*.

in Malaysia is that one is Muslim. Race, on the other hand, although also a culturally constructed category, emphasizes easily recognized physical characteristics (such as skin color) and tends to rely on a folk theory of biological origins that offers a comprehensive accounting of all human types. Often such theories have a mythological base, such as the idea that "races" of the world originated with the different sons of Noah.

Anthropology has had a tempestuous relationship with race. In the nineteenth century anthropologists were deeply engaged in trying to discover a measurable "scientific" basis for human racial categories. Millions of measurements were taken, particularly of the skull, in an attempt to define races "anthropometrically"—all in vain since there turned out to be as much variability within populations as there was between races. Nonetheless, the motives of many of these anthropologists were deeply racist, and their conclusions were adopted by eugenicists, Nazis, and others who sought a scientific justification for hatred. In the twentieth century anthropologists, particularly the Boasians, took the lead in discrediting racialist theories. Boas regarded it as an important public mission for anthropology, and one of his best students, Ruth Benedict, coined the term "racism" in a 1940 book written for popular consumption.

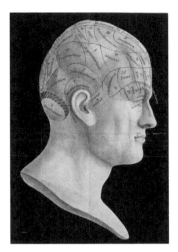

In their attempts to discover a scientific basis for human racial categories, some nineteenth-century anthropologists took millions of measurements, particularly of the human skull, in an attempt to define races anthropometrically. Their deeply racist conclusions were adopted by, among others, eugenicists and Nazis. This lithograph from around 1834 shows a phrenological labeling of a human skull with division markings including "destructiveness" and "secretiveness."

If we are likely to see in ethnicity an identity based on shared blood, and in race an identity based on shared physical characteristics, in nationalism we see shared heritage and experience taken as the basis of the state. Typically, nationalism involves the idea that a group has a claim to political autonomy by virtue of its common language, unique customs, and shared origin. Because almost every modern state includes people of diverse cultural backgrounds, nationalism is often the political expression of a particular ethnicity or race. The pervasiveness of nationalism in the modern world is such that we often use "nation" and "state" interchangeably. However, nationalism can exist in the absence of an established state (or, as in the case of the Kurds, despite being spread among several states) and the state—a centralized and bureaucratized political unit whose control extends across a given territory—can be founded on principles other than nationalistic ones. Even in the many modern states whose populations patently do not share a language, customs, or heritage, a great many resources are expended on programs that promote such things, "inventing," as it were, a common tradition. In such cases, groups that do not share the national culture are classified as ethnic or racial minorities.

Nation-states that traditionally have been quite effective in promoting a vision of themselves as made up of "one people, one language, and one culture" have been increasingly challenged by such groups, as these latter articulate their own national aspirations. Another challenge to established national identities comes from transnational groups, as new technologies of travel and communication have allowed the creation of social ties that span state boundaries to a degree not possible in previous eras. Mixtec communities, for example, no longer exist in just one place—a rural village in the mountains of Oaxaca—but in several different places, including Mexico City, Baja California, North Carolina, and Canada, with members circulating among these various localities. This binational and urban as well as rural residence has coincided with the emergence of labor unions and other organizations that are based on an inclusive Mixtec identity, rather than membership in particular communities. These groups have begun to promote the interests of the Mixtec wherever they happen to be, and will mobilize resources available to them in one place—Mexico—in order to achieve their goals in another—the United States. What all this will mean for succeeding generations in both their new and old homes remains to be seen, but is an active front for ethnographic research.

If nationalist ideologies are being challenged by the emergence of transnational communities such as the one described above, then so too is the anthropological concept of culture, which operates with a similar assumption—that the world is divided into groups of people who share customs and speak a common language. In developing his concept of culture, Boas explicitly drew upon the nationalist project of the nineteenth-century German historicist tradition, which used the idea of *Geist*—the spirit of a people—to explain what it was that made the peoples of Prussia, Hanover, Bavaria, and so on a nation in the absence of a unifying state.

As we pointed out earlier, the Boasian vision of culture has given way to a more contingent and less circumscribed focus on meaning, not limited to tradition. Although written in broader and finer strokes, kinship, ethnicity, race, nation, and culture are a family of related concepts, founded on what Robert Lowie called a "consciousness of kind."

"Consciousness of Kind"

Consciousness of kind does not have to rely on an ideology of kinship. Anthropologists have usually defined groups that are not based on kinship in a negative or residual way (for example, "nonkinship" groups) probably because basing group identity upon an idea of shared descent, to whatever extent real or imagined, seems universally to be the most potent basis for communal solidarity. But these different ways of regulating group life are not opposed or mutually exclusive. Even in societies that are quintessentially kinship-based, one can find important groupings based on age and gender that may bridge the divisions between kin-based groups. In some traditional African societies, for example, males were grouped together in "age-sets" for purposes of ritual, warfare, and other civic responsibilities. Religious congregations, such as the *zar* cults of eastern Africa, can provide an important cross-cutting identity for women, too.

Perhaps the most important kind of social group not based on kinship is the community. To be sure, there are communities primarily organized around kin groups, like the villages of many Amazonian peoples, which are both physically and ideologically constituted of opposing *moieties* (two parts, but not necessarily halves) composed of kin groups. But most of the world's communities are formed on the basis of simple coresidence and the daily interaction proximity requires. Much can be made of the differences between village life and urban life—and, indeed, there is a subdiscipline of anthropology explicitly devoted to the latter—but at their core communities command an identification and allegiance that is rooted in the shared history and shared experience of its members, an experience of place and a celebration of what the German philosopher Martin Heidegger called "homeliness." Allegiance to one's home or region, while lacking the ideology of shared blood implicit in ethnicity, may entail a sense that one is profoundly shaped by one's surroundings and that anyone who shares those surroundings is similarly shaped. A sense of place can be extraordinarily powerful, as among the Western Apache, where particular features of the landscape are named to encode stories with powerful moral lessons. Similarly, Italians are not alone in feeling a greater sense of identity and a deeper allegiance to their city or region than to the nation-state. As Durkheim predicted, collective representations are often crucial to creating feelings of solidarity in larger communities that are otherwise highly fractionalized. We vividly remember the qualitative difference in community feeling in Philadelphia in 1980 when the Phillies won the baseball championship for the first time in over half a century.

There are, of course, a wide variety of nonkin groups that fall below the level of community or, for that matter, that extend across many communities. Religious congregations are an extraordinarily powerful kind of group, which may be composed of a segment of a physical community, or may entirely constitute a community (as in the case of monasteries), or may extend across several communities and be linked to many other congregations worldwide. Religious institutions such as the Catholic Church are among the first and most important transnational organizations. Voluntary organizations may operate in a similar way. Clubs, service organizations, secret societies, and the like all provide a means for individuals to gather, interact, and share a consciousness of kind based

A wide variety of nonkin groups fall below the level of community or may extend across many communities. Religious congregations, such as monasteries, may entirely constitute a community. This photograph from between 1898 and 1914 shows Franciscan monks at the American Colony in Jerusalem.

on more or less autonomous personal choices. For example, in Java and elsewhere in Southeast Asia, rotating credit associations are very popular. In these groups of neighbors and friends everyone contributes a sum each week and one member, chosen in turn at random, gets to take home all the money. These associations provide a motive for savings and they are highly prized for the sociability and sense of communal support that goes with regular participation. Other kinds of group may be more overtly concerned with power and political economy. Labor unions, for example, depend on a consciousness of kind based on the common experience of working in a particular trade or industry and on a perception of common interests, particularly vis-à-vis management and the owners of the means of production.

The phenomenon of social class is like these other forms of consciousness of kind insofar as it does not rely on an ideology of shared blood. And certainly class is important as a kind of identity that cuts across other forms of social organization. At the same time, class does not require the same sort of overt membership that a club, or a union, or a religious affiliation requires. Class can be as much a political abstraction or sociological construct as a social phenomenon with a specifiable structure and content. No one would deny the reality of social class, particularly in industrialized societies. For Karl Marx class was the only social grouping that reflected politico-economic reality, regardless of whether its members recognized their common interests and identity. For Marx, one's social class was defined by one's relationship to "ownership of the means of production," from which all other social dynamics flowed. Others have emphasized the means by which class distinctions are made or how individuals or groups can move up or down the social ladder; these are a particular concern of sociologists. Anthropologists have tended to be interested in the cultural dimensions of class, as, for example, in the way Pierre Bourdieu has described the accumulation and expenditure of "cultural capital" as creating and maintaining class distinctions (see Chapter 3). By and large, anthropologists have used a larger number of more specific analytical categories, such as "patron-client" relations or "relationships of dependency."

Transnationalism and Globalization

Classical anthropology depended on a vision of the "Other" as comprising unique and coherent cultures, living in more or less splendid isolation from the rest of the world. Anthropologists have always recognized this vision as a convenient, if somewhat romantic, fiction, and there have always been anthropologists interested in contact between cultures, the diffusion of cultural traits, and the like. Still, we have tended to talk about cultures as if they were well bounded and well integrated even when we may have recognized otherwise. In the concluding decades of the twentieth century, however, new technologies have vastly accelerated both the speed and the volume of flows of people and information, across regional and international boundaries. Eager as ever to seize a serendipitous opportunity, anthropologists have recently begun to study these flows with interest, and the emergence of new social formations has always been a stimulus to model building in the social sciences. This has posed considerable methodological challenges, as the lone ethnographer of classical anthropology cannot hope to encompass processes of a global nature. It is one thing to live in a village community for a year or two, getting to know the dynamics of social life in a relatively circumscribed setting. It is altogether another to follow the lives of people from, for example, refugee camps to a dozen immigrant communities spread across the globe. There is no doubt that people and information are coursing through the world at rates never seen before. Whether this acceleration will produce qualitative differences in human life or merely quantitative ones is harder to know.

After a century that has gone from Sarajevo to Sarajevo, it is surely premature to pronounce the death of nationalism or the nation-state. But there do seem to be a variety of forces—cultural, economic, and political—that if not threatening the autonomy and authority of nation-states are at the least redefining what it means to be a citizen. These forces are most evident in the growth of new economic processes: organizations such as the International Monetary Fund and the World Bank can have an enormous impact on the economies of nations; wild fluctuations of stock markets in one part of the world are triggered by boom and bust in other parts. In spite of these profound effects, none of these institutions appears to be accountable to any government or nation. Multinational corporations are, if anything, less accountable to national governments and seem to be developing a kind of international culture. Anthropologists have taken a keen interest in the ways that these global processes have affected the peoples we have traditionally studied. Studies of labor migrations, refugees, and the policies and politics of national governments with respect to indigenous peoples fill anthropological journals today. Other anthropologists have become interested in the globalization of culture itself: the emergence of a set of hybrid, deterritorialized practices and images surrounding consumption, epitomized by fast-food chains, world fairs, sporting events, cinemas, and tourist destinations.

It is important to remember, however, that the processes of globalization and transnationalism we see today are but an extension of processes in human history that have been in place for a very long time. No culture has ever been completely isolated. A classic case in point is that of the Plains Indians (Sioux, Omaha, Crow, Cheyenne, Shoshone, etc.), whose nomadic style of buffalo hunting and dashing mounted warfare depended entirely on the introduction of the horse to North America by Spanish colonizers in the sixteenth century. Similarly, our friend Carl Hoffman conducted research in the interior of the island of Borneo among hunter-gatherers called Punan, and came to the conclusion that many of those who had been assumed to be hunter-gatherers through the centuries in fact had originated among agricultural peoples who had taken to a foraging economy to acquire forest products such as gutta percha, edible bird's nests, and beeswax to meet the demands of markets as far away as China. While Hoffman's conclusions are controversial, there is little doubt that the peoples anthropologists study have long

Today's processes of globalization and transnationalism are extensions of processes that have existed for a very long time. The Bornean people called the Punan, for example, who have been known as hunter-gatherers over the centuries, in fact originated in an agricultural people who began to forage for products to sell in lands as far away as China. Two Punan hunters are shown here in a photograph taken in 1991.

been involved in a complex, worldwide division of labor. Transnational organizations, only partially accountable to national governments, are also nothing new: we have already mentioned the Catholic Church as one centuries-old example.

Similarly, we must regard the idea of the emergence of a single, homogenized global culture with considerable skepticism. The student of a colleague once observed, "Hey, they wear blue jeans and we eat salsa. It's all the same, isn't it?" In fact it seems to us that these superficial similarities often mask profound cultural differences, differences that may operate at a deep structural level. The expansion of global markets and the reproduction of local identities and values need not be contradictory processes. One might think, for example, that Japan's adoption of industrial capitalism and liberal democracy might have completely transformed the basis of its social organization. But Japanese anthropologist Chie Nakane has noted that while in the West there is a tendency for people and groups to be organized in horizontal strata that cut across local sites of community or enterprise (for example, as in labor unions), in Japan there is a pronounced preference for a kind of vertical organization that cuts across strata of class or specialization. In other words, an American assembly-line worker at Ford is more likely to feel a consciousness of kind with an assembly-line worker at General Motors than with a member of Ford's management; the same can be said for the managers. But according to Nakane, auto workers at Honda in Japan feel a greater sense of identity with their fellow workers and managers at Honda than with their counterparts at Toyota. The Japanese tend to stress a familial ideology in the organization of industrial enterprises, including a sense of hierarchical top-to-bottom integration, and employ a variety of collective representations—company flags, anthems, uniforms, and so on—to strengthen loyalty and obedience. This, Nakane argues, is a characteristically *Japanese* way of doing things, and while this way of doing things has adapted to industrialism it has also begun to modify the face of industrial organization. As we were writing this chapter, the newspapers reported on a Japanese corporate executive who had committed suicide because he felt responsible for the suffering inflicted on workers as a result of "downsizing" in the wake of a recent business recession. It is hard to imagine an American or European executive feeling more than a passing pang of remorse over what he or she would regard as an unpleasant economic necessity, much less resorting to so characteristically Japanese a response as protest suicide.

SIX

A Feast in Nuyoo: People and Their Things

●

MOST DAYS NUYOO IS A SLEEPY little place, with people leaving early in the morning to work in their fields and gardens and not returning until late afternoon. In sharp contrast are days when fiestas are held. Nuyootecos maintain an elaborate cult of the saints, with twenty-four separate feasts celebrated annually. Some of these feasts last for as long as three days. For important saints, such as the town patron, Santiago, markets are held, basketball tournaments are organized, elaborate processions are staged, and a priest comes to town to offer a Mass. Key actors in all of this are the *mayordomos*, a man and a woman, usually husband and wife, who are charged with organizing the cult activities and providing as many as nine separate meals for the hundreds of participants in the celebration. Because no household can possibly acquire and prepare all the food needed to feed

The flows of goods and services among people provide a starting point for examining social cohesion and competition, power and prestige, and hierarchy and solidarity. In this photograph taken sometime between 1880 and 1897, a woman prepares tortillas in Aguacalientes, Mexico.

so many guests, Nuyootecos rely on a system of reciprocal exchange, called *saa sa'a*, to finance the fiesta. For the one to two years before they hold their own fiesta a couple will attend the fiestas sponsored by other Nuyootecos, making contributions of tortillas (usually a basket of sixty, a standard measure), beans, liquor, and cash, which are used to provide meals for fiesta guests. When the date of their own fiesta approaches, the couple expects that what they have given will be returned in kind. At the same time other Nuyootecos with fiestas to sponsor in the future will arrive with foodstuffs, liquor, and cash, which the sponsoring couple will return when their fiestas come around. *Saa sa'a* thus allows Nuyootecos to accumulate large amounts of fiesta items and spread the cost of this accumulation over a long period of time. It also links each household to many other households in a complex cycle of exchanges.

Fiestas are usually happy times, and people will linger for days afterward at the house of the sponsors to gossip, joke, and eat the leftover food. But one fiesta John attended was quite different. It began well enough, but midway through, something happened to make everyone tense. During one of the meals someone found a clump of hair in the tortilla she was eating. This hair, people speculated, had come from a corpse, and the incident was widely believed to be an attempt at witchcraft. What made it particularly unsettling for the Nuyootecos, and cast such a pall over the fiesta, was that they interpreted it to be directed not at the woman who found the hair in the tortilla, but at all of them.

During Nuyooteco fiestas, something special happens with the food the sponsors accumulate. As partners drop off their contributions, the items are counted and placed among those brought by other participants. At this point no one pays any attention to the source of a particular item and the contributions are purposely mixed together, so that in the meals and other distributions made during the fiestas, people receive food made by many different people. Nuyootecos explicitly compare this store of food to the household larder, and say by eating the fiesta food it is as if they were members of the same household. In other words, people arrive at the fiesta as members of separate households, but through the sharing of food are transformed into one household. Nuyootecos in fact often characterize themselves as "people who eat from the same tortilla," an image of unity based upon the sharing that takes place among household members. What made the hair in the tortilla so disturbing was that in poisoning the fiesta food the witch was able to subvert the normal meanings of the exchanges and attack the whole community. Moreover, since few outsiders attend Nuyooteco fiestas, the witch must have been one of their own.

Clearly there is quite a bit more than cold calculations of profit and loss in Nyooteco exchanges. This is not to say that there is no financial utility in *saa sa'a*. Through its rotation of credit and debt, *saa sa'a* is in fact a very efficient way to finance large lump-sum expenditures. But the fiesta exchanges also show that people use things to maintain, create, and, in the case of the hair in the tortilla, transform their relationships with one another. Anthropologists like John have long taken the flows of goods and services among people in exchange networks as a starting point for examining social cohesion and competition, power and prestige, hierarchy and solidarity. In some cases it seems that the financial utility of such exchanges is almost nil, with the whole point being what the exchange says about the social bonds that exist between the groups or the individuals participating in the transaction. But let's not be overly romantic in viewing Nuyooteco reciprocity. Although called "gift exchange," it is certainly not what we would call a free gift, since people definitely expect to be repaid. Still, the focus of the transaction is not profit at the expense of others, and the Mixtec would be horrified if anyone suggested that it was.

An anecdote from Peter's fieldwork may help to illustrate some of the ways that the principle of reciprocity both obligates the recipient of a gift and may be used as a political resource. When visiting Bima Town, Peter and his wife Anne would stay at the home of a local political leader, Haji M. Djafar Amyn. Haji Djafar Amyn and his wife, Haja Syarafiah, were extraordinarily generous hosts, frequently and over a long time. Naturally, Peter and Anne felt obliged to reciprocate their hospitality and on several occasions invited their lowland hosts to visit them at their home in Donggo. After many such invitations, the Bimanese couple accepted, and made the difficult trip up to Doro Ntika. Folks in the

Haji M. Djafar Amyn (right) and Haja Syarafiah (center holding baby) with their family. This Bimanese couple were dear friends and generous hosts to Peter and Anne when they would visit Bima Town, but for obscure reasons H. M. Djafar Amyn refused to eat at a feast given for him in Donggo. He was an active participant in the struggle for Indonesian independence, the head of the local education and culture ministry, and president of the regency legislature. Haja Syarafiah was the daughter of a Bimanese noble and a woman of grace, intelligence, and energy.

village were very excited at the prospect of entertaining an eminent local political figure—Haji Djafar Amyn was head of the Bimanese legislature at the time—and made elaborate preparations for a feast to be held in his honor. The Dou Donggo pride themselves on their hospitality, often saying that if a householder has only one chicken to his name, he will slaughter it to feed even a guest who arrives unexpectedly. When H. Djafar Amyn arrived at the feast, however, he sat and enjoyed conversation with everyone, but he declined to eat anything. His wife was embarrassed, Peter and Anne were confused, but the villagers were distraught. "If he won't eat anything, how can we ask him to help us?" they complained. To this day, Peter and Anne are uncertain as to why H. Djafar Amyn wouldn't eat. Peter suspects that he was afraid the meat might not have been *halal* (suitable for Muslims to eat), but also wonders if he may simply have wished to avoid the obligations of reciprocity that accepting food might have created. In any case, this anecdote illustrates nicely the universal power of "the gift," both in Peter and Anne's felt need to reciprocate the hospitality they had received and in the villagers' failed attempt to use hospitality as a political resource.

The Politics of Exchange

Reciprocal transactions are not always perfectly symmetric, nor do they always imply equality between giver and receiver. In many instances the giver is seen as superior to the receiver in moral if not material terms, enjoying that superiority until the gift has been repaid or, if possible, bettered. Reciprocating a gift exactly can be seen as a hostile act, since it effectively terminates a relationship built on exchange. At the same time, we probably have all experienced a kind of discomfort when in exchanging gifts, say as at Christmas, someone gives us a much more lavish gift than we have for him or her. Of course this doesn't apply when social relations are already highly asymmetric: an employee does not feel uncomfortable when an employer gives a nicer present than the employee returns. So the social relations between the giver and the receiver are crucial in deciding the meaning of the gift.

The politics of reciprocity indicate that exchanges may be motivated by something other than the bonds of communal solidarity. The competitive exchanges that took place among Native American groups on the northwest coast of the United States and Canada in the nineteenth century are a case in point. During a celebration called a *potlatch* a contending group

Competitive gift exchanges among Native American groups of the northwest coast of the United States and Canada, called potlatches, allowed a contending group to demonstrate its superior economic and social power by giving its rival such a large gift that it could not easily be repaid. This watercolor by James Gilchrist Swan (1818–1900), an Indian agent authorized to interact with Native Americans on behalf of the US government, shows the Klallam people at a potlatch at Port Townsend, Washington State.

would try to give its rival such a large gift that it could not be easily repaid. This would demonstrate their superior economic and social power. When these societies experienced a massive influx of manufactured goods as payment for their participation in the fur trade, the frequency and size of these competitive exchanges increased to the point where potlatching was defined by some observers as "warring with property." People who would not normally have had access to the goods necessary to make large exchanges were suddenly able to make crushingly large gifts to groups and individuals above them in the hierarchy. Before being shut down by the colonial governments, potlatch gifts reached thousands of blankets, tons of food, and vast quantities of local valuables which might be destroyed as well as given to rivals in an effort to demonstrate the wealth and superiority of the givers.

Another way this kind of asymmetry works out is in relations of dependence, where people are not able to reciprocate at all with material goods. In such instances they may be able to reciprocate only with obedience, deference, or loyalty. Where relations of dependence are built into a society's socioeconomic system the result can be what anthropologists call "clientage," that is, relations between wealthy or powerful patrons and those who depend on them for material resources or protection. In its least degrading form patron-client relations retain a sense of noblesse oblige on the part of the patron and a genuine loyalty on the part of the client. In the old-fashioned ward politics of American cities, political patrons provided civil service jobs and services for their immigrant clients in exchange for their votes. In more exploitative circumstances, clientage can amount to little more than extortion on the part of the patron and, at its extreme, dependence can result in a particular kind of slavery, where, because people have become so impoverished that they can no longer support themselves they give themselves over as servants to people who can.

As these examples illustrate, it is difficult to talk about real economies without taking into account a number of other aspects of the society in question, since economic relations are inextricably embedded in the political and social. Part of the problem is that we are so involved in capitalist economies we tend to assume that the only kind of "economic" behavior is that of buying and selling in the market, and the only context for such activities is the nation-state. But as we have seen, reciprocity can be an equally significant economic principle in human life and a full understanding of economic life in many societies would have to take account of a range of nonmarket transactions such as marriage payments, gift exchanges, tribute, and sacrifice, and specialized institutions such as clan organizations, caste, slavery, or kingship.

Production

Looking at people and their things in terms of exchange and the social relations that surround it is one important way anthropologists have approached economy. Another important way of looking at the economy is through the lens of production. Karl Marx saw our drive to create by transforming nature as the essence of humanity. This in turn led him to classify societies based on their productive relations: primitive, feudal, oriental, capitalist, and socialist. An important school of neo-evolutionary anthropology has produced its own evolutionary typology based on how people organize themselves to produce, the technologies they have available to them, and the environment in which they operate. According to this classification, there are four basic patterns of human society. There are *foraging societies*, in which people live in relatively small, flexible,

One school of neo-evolutionary anthropology, which organizes people according to how they organize themselves to produce, the technologies they have available, and the environment in which they operate, categorizes people into foraging societies, tribal societies, chiefdoms, and states. This ca. 1924 photograph shows a Pomo woman from northern California demonstrating a foraging technique, using a seed beater to gather seeds into a burden basket.

nomadic groups, possess a subsistence technology designed for hunting and gathering wild foods, and range over a relatively large territory. There are *tribal societies*, in which people live in larger groups (often articulated by ties of descent), possess a technology that allows them to practice some form of horticulture (such as digging sticks, axes for cutting back the forest), and unlike foraging societies (in which group size and composition tracks environmental variability), have a capacity to store and preserve food so that they can somewhat insulate themselves against seasonal fluctuations in food supply. The third type of society is the *chiefdom*, in which people are divided into ranked social groups based on proximity of descent from a noble or sacred ancestor and in which commoners pay some kind of tribute to the nobles. Chiefly societies tend to maintain larger populations and may employ technologies such as irrigation which, while costly, allow the population to produce food crops more intensively. Finally there is the *state*, which is complexly stratified, often divided into urban and rural components. The rural component, or peasant sector, produces surpluses with a highly developed agricultural technology to support the cities, which in turn maintain a highly complex division of labor with many different kinds of craft specialists. While neo-evolutionary archaeologists caution us not to reify these into rigid evolutionary stages, this typology provides a rough classificatory tool that anthropologists of many different persuasions continue to use.

Consumption

Why do people want the things they want? An economist's answer would begin with a list of basic human needs (food, shelter, and so on). It might then discuss a particular good's scarcity, the dynamics of supply and demand, and how its consumption marks the consumer as a wealthy or important individual. Psychological explanations might also be invoked. But other factors also enter into consumption decisions. In the United States, retail sales, one of the most important measures of the economy, peak around Christmastime. The economy of Turkey, where a different sacred calendar reigns, would not have the same periodicity. Even as basic a human need as food is inflected by cultural factors. Thus the Spanish *conquistadores*, when they first arrived in the New World, believed that even though there was an abundance of maize, game, fruits, and vegetables, they were being starved since they could not obtain wine, wheat, or olive oil—elements they believed to be essential to a healthy diet. In the case of conspicuous consumption, people want things so they can show they are not like anyone else, or at least not like most people. But as any good advertising executive can tell you, the sale of things ranging from clothing to cars is driven by consumers' wishes to signal that they belong to some groups and do not belong to others.

Consumption does not come naturally, then, but is something we have to learn, and what one society learns to value might not be the same as what another society learns to value. A good example of this involves what we might call, following Alfred Gell, "exotic consumerism." John was giving one of his Mixtec friends, who had been living in Tennessee, a ride back to Mexico in John's car. On the day they were to leave, the friend showed up with three television sets, a hair dryer, a chain saw, a gasoline lantern, two boom boxes, a microphone, and sundry other electronic equipment, all used and most of it not working very well (if at all). After spending quite some time trying to fit the load in the car, John turned to his friend in frustration and said, "I can't believe you want to bring all this junk back with you, especially since your town doesn't have electricity." Later, when John visited his friend's house in an isolated area of the Mixteca, he saw all these items in the house, with most of them set up on tables and shelves almost like museum pieces. These were meant to be artifacts of the man's travels, and they were meant to display his ability to consume Western electronic gear. Six months later John gave the same friend a ride back to the United States. This time it was John who filled up the car, with pottery, bark paintings, woven rugs and blankets, straw baskets, and papier maché figures. His Mixtec friend, after spending eight hours balancing a large pot on his lap, got out of the car and using almost the same language John had used six months earlier, said in frustration, "I can't believe you bought all this junk to bring back with you, especially since you never use any of these pots for cooking!'

Money and Markets

"Money," as Cyndi Lauper reminds us, "money changes everything." In the politics of reciprocity and exchange of simple societies the "economic" value of a transaction is subordinated to the social relationship created by the transaction. In an important sense, each transaction is as unique as the individuals entering into the exchange. Bronislaw Malinowski observed the Trobriand Islanders engaged in an elaborate "ring" of exchanges with other Melanesian islanders whereby individuals traveled long distances to exchange specific kinds

Bargaining over the price of duck eggs at a market in Yogyakarta, Java.

of goods with lifelong trading partners. As the items circulated in this "*kula* ring" the history of the transactions and of their previous owners circulated with them, so that each exchange and each object acquired a unique life story. Money and market exchanges, the foundation blocks of modern economies, have precisely the opposite effect, and quite deliberately so. Reducing values to a common, standardized, convertible standard immensely increases the efficiency of exchanges both in speed and volume. When the token of exchange has no intrinsic value in relation to its worth—as is the case with paper money—then the transition of exchange to an abstraction is almost complete. And newer technologies, such as electronic funds transfers, complete the process.

Money is sometimes taken as an example of what Anthony Giddens has called "disembedding mechanisms" that constitute the "dynamism of modernity." By turning value into symbolic tokens produced and managed by expert systems, money erases the local particularities of production and exchange. But before we slip into another one of those traditional/modern dichotomies, keep in mind that this transition is not as complete as we might assume. "Modern" currencies, like primitive valuables, are also symbols. The dollar bill, for example, portrays an "apical ancestor," George Washington, uses ritual language, Latin, makes references to the original federation of states that gave rise to the United States, and repeatedly invokes God. What it does—and most currencies do this—is symbolize the strength and stability of the state that has issued it. In an era of huge trade deficits, the dollar's high exchange ratio relative to other currencies only serves to underscore the fact that the value of a currency is based on trust and perceptions. Moreover, in capitalist economies, many forms of restricted use moneys exist, such as subway tokens, gift certificates, coupons, and food stamps, which are often issued with the warning that it is illegal to convert them into other currencies. And even in the United States money cannot buy everything—witness the outrage caused by the auction Web site that recently offered body organs and religious credentials for sale.

Although modern currencies are not as unique as social theorists sometimes make them out to be, this does not negate the profound effects the transition from a largely subsistence economy to a market economy has on people's lives. Donggo was in the midst of such a transition when Peter conducted fieldwork in the early 1980s. Until that time the people of Doro Ntika had devoted the vast majority of their labor and productive effort to growing the food they ate and making the other things they needed. Everyone in the village farmed land; every woman was a competent weaver and made her family's clothes; every man was a competent sawyer and carpenter who, with the help of his kin and friends, built the house he lived in. In recent years, however, as education became available other kinds of opportunities opened up and some young people from the village became schoolteachers, police officers, and nurses. Parents were eager for their children to have such opportunities and were also eager to have access to the cash incomes such occupations provided and thereby have access to luxuries and consumer goods that only money can buy. But educating a child also requires cash money. For that and other reasons many Dou Donggo have shifted a good deal of their labor to cultivating crops such as peanuts and soybeans, which are not consumed by the farmer but are sold in lowland markets for cash. Men are increasingly likely to leave the village during the dry season to work as laborers on government building projects. While a shift to a cash economy offers great advantages, such as access to consumer goods and medicine, it also exposes people to new risks: if they invest too much of their resources in cash crops they put themselves at the mercy of market forces far beyond their control as the prices of their crops respond to global fluctuations in supply and demand. They may also end up worse off in nutritional terms, as a range of traditional subsistence crops is replaced by mono-crop cultivation. Beyond this, participation in international labor markets may increase the domestic burdens of some, as women and old people take the place of migrating men and younger people in the fields, effectively forcing some to work a double shift. Because other members of the migrant's household assume responsibility for basic subsistence needs, the migrant's wages can be kept artificially low, as they do not have to cover the cost of maintaining a family.

SEVEN

A Drought in Bima: People and Their Gods

•

THE DOU DONGGO SHARE THE eastern part of Sumbawa Island with the Bimanese, a much larger group who speak the same language and share much history with the Dou Donggo, but who are fervent followers of Islam. The climate of the region is characterized by sharply differentiated wet and dry seasons. In the wet season it rains nearly every day; in the dry season the island is a desert. Since both Bimanese and the Dou Donggo depend on rain for their crops, the timing of the wet season's arrival is crucial. In 1982 the normal time for the arrival of the rains passed without a drop. As the rainless days stretched on, people both in the Donggo highlands and in the Bima lowlands became more and more anxious, especially since many of

An offering to the spirits of the mountain. Ama Balo makes an offering of rice wine, rice, betel, tobacco, and a chicken to the spirits of the *sou*, the place on the mountain where the community has planted swidden rice. The offering, placed on a rude tray in the fork of a branch erected in the soil, is intended to propitiate the spirits of the place so that the rice may grow and be harvested in peace.

them were subsistence farmers who would literally starve if the rains failed altogether. The differing responses of the two groups to this crisis are both fascinating and instructive. The Muslim lowlanders declared a day of fasting and prayer, assembling in the Grand Mosque in the center of Bima Town to beseech Allah to give them rain. In the Donggo highlands, however, a group of respected village elders, who were leaders of the community and ritual specialists, went out into the bush to a particular mountain spring. There they cleaned the accumulated debris from around the mouth of the spring and made an offering of rice wine, rice, betel, tobacco, and a chicken sacrificed at the spot, all of which were intended to propitiate mischievous spirits who were stopping up the normal flow of water and the coming of the rains. In the event, a few days after both these efforts the rainy season arrived and crops were, if anything, more plentiful than usual.

This story can tell us a good deal about the nature of religion. Let's begin by characterizing exactly how the two responses to this crisis differ. For the Muslims, the annual rains were, like all good things, a gift from Allah, the single and all-powerful high God. Human beings are dependent on God's goodwill, which in turn may depend on their behavior. Allah is, by definition, wholly otherworldly, formless, and antecedent to all existence on Earth. For the Dou Donggo, on the other hand, the rains are part of a natural order and, if this order is left unperturbed, they come in due course and are sufficient to allow human beings to pursue their lives in peace and plenty. The mischievous spirits who interfere with this natural process have their origin in human birth: they are formed from the placenta discarded in the bush after a woman has given birth to a child. They are, as the Dou Donggo say, "the part of us that did not become human," and they are envious of us because of this. That is why they sometimes act so mischievously and why they can be placated with the things any human would want: a bit of food and drink, a chew of betel, and a cigarette. The spirits are, in short, parochial, numerous, and, despite their origins, in many ways quite human.

The comparison becomes even more interesting when we note that until very recently the Bimanese had a semifeudal society in which a sultan at least in theory owned all the land and, in effect, all the people in it. An ordinary person depended on the sultan or his aristocratic subordinates for the very means of production for his livelihood. The relationship between ruler and ruled was very much characterized as the relationship between a father and his children—a metaphor not coincidentally also applied to the relationship between God and humans. The sultan, moreover, was no ordinary human, but royalty, and quite unlike common folk, from whom he differs by nature and by birth. Dou Donggo society, in contrast, has always been an egalitarian one, relations among neighbors being compared to relations among siblings. Subsistence depends on the cultivation of land communally owned by the village as a whole, not by a single sovereign. Kin and neighbors are both help and trouble in one's life. So although the connection is not explicitly made, religion and society are both models *of* each other and models *for* each other.

These parallels between cosmological propositions and social arrangements have suggested a complex interplay between religion and society. Anthropological approaches to religion, in contrast to those that focus on theology or the philosophical positions of religious thinkers, have tended to be concerned with the everyday practice of religion and how it connects to the rest of social life. Early in the twentieth century Émile Durkheim suggested that it was in religion that one finds basic social categorizations and that it was through cosmology that people represented their society to themselves, thus indicating that there was a causal connection between society and religion. A crude way of putting this idea is that religious rituals are instances of "society worshipping itself," while at the same time creating intense personal communal experiences that confirm social solidarity. Other scholars, taking a less deterministic approach, have emphasized the way religion mobilizes groups and individuals to get through crises and other difficult events. In *rites of passage*, for example, the problematic transition of individuals from one kind of social identity to another is effected through

Rites of passage, or the transition of individuals from one kind of social identity to another, are marked by some of the most elaborate rituals in a society. This member of the Baining, a Papua New Guinean tribe, is participating in the fire dance, which is used as part of the initiation of young men into adulthood.

what are often the most elaborate rituals practiced in a society. Arnold van Gennep, a student of European folklore, suggested we think of society as a large house with many rooms, each room symbolizing a different social status. Rites of passage move people from one room to another, allowing them to shed an old status and acquire a new one. In the course of these transitions, ceremonies are held which are designed to remove individuals from the old status and bestow upon them the insignia of the new one, often employing metaphors of death and rebirth to describe the process. While "on the threshold," individuals have a special status, not one thing or another. This status is usually marked by the wearing of special clothing, alterations of physical appearance, the suffering of austerities, and the like. All societies have some ritual means for helping people through transitions in life—sometimes these are called *life crisis rituals*—which may or may not invoke the sacred. We are familiar with religious rituals that move us from being unborn to childhood, as in a christening; from children to adults, as in the Jewish bar mitzvah; or from unmarried to married, as in weddings; or from living to dead, as in funerals. Secular rites of passage are also familiar to us, as in graduations or inaugurations.

Belief Systems

In looking at both the Bimanese and Dou Donggo responses to drought and at the ways rites of passage help people through major changes in their lives, it seems apparent that one thing religion or belief helps us do is deal with problems of human life that are significant, persistent, and intolerable. One important way in which religious beliefs accomplish this is by providing a set of ideas about how and why the world is put together that allows people to accommodate anxieties and deal with misfortune. In complex societies these belief systems are highly elaborate, divided among several social institutions, and are often articulated and codified: think, for example, of the different ways in which science, religion, and "common sense" explain the death of a child in a road accident. In many of the societies anthropologists traditionally have studied, such beliefs are often more diffuse and uninstitutionalized, often being characterized as beliefs in magic or witchcraft. It is important not to view such beliefs as irrational or mere superstition. In *Magic, Witchcraft, and Oracles Among the Azande*, British social anthropologist E. E. Evans-Pritchard described a people who regard all misfortune as a consequence of witchcraft. In a famous example Evans-Pritchard tells of how several Azande were killed when a granary doorway collapsed. The Azande attributed their deaths to witchcraft. Evans-Pritchard pointed out that the doorway had been weakened by termites. "We understand that," he was told. "But why did those particular people happen to be sitting in the doorway at just the moment when it collapsed? *That's* the witchcraft!" Westerners would ascribe the misfortune in this to "coincidence" or "chance," which, when you think of it, is no explanation at all. Accepting the premise of witchcraft as a reality, the Azande explanation is not only logical and rational; it provides a moral meaning for what has happened. Moreover, the Azande have a highly developed set of oracular procedures for determining who the source of the witchcraft is and in precolonial days had regular legal procedures for dealing with murderous witches.

Religious Movements

What happens when established beliefs no longer provide an adequate explanation for life's problems? Often the societies anthropologists deal with, subordinated to colonial and neocolonial governments, experience such sudden and overwhelming changes that traditional religious beliefs are unable to encompass the resulting dislocations. In such situations an intense religious movement may arise, often led by a prophet, who seeks to provide an explanation for and a solution to the problems the society faces. Called *millenary movements*, these are led by individuals who speak with the authority of the sacred, something which may allow them to introduce far-reaching religious and secular changes as part of the solution to the crisis people face. In the anthropological literature such movements are well reported for native North America, such as the Long House Religion among the Seneca, an Iroquois tribe of New York, which began in the late eighteenth century, and in Melanesia, with the emergence of "cargo

Millenary movements are intense religious movements, often led by a prophet, that attempt to explain and provide a solution for a crisis faced by a group of people. In Melanesia, the sudden arrival of technologically advanced Allied soldiers during World War II—and their just as sudden departure after the war ended—caused great psychological upheaval among the technologically simple people of the interior. This US Army Signal Corps photograph of native stretcher bearers in New Guinea, resting en route from carrying American wounded from the front lines to hospitals in the rear, was probably taken in 1942.

cults" in the late nineteenth and twentieth centuries. American Indians had, of course, suffered the loss of their lands, their livelihoods, and as much as nine-tenths of their population. In Melanesia, the sudden arrival of unimaginably wealthy and technologically advanced Allied soldiers during World War II, and then their equally sudden disappearance at its end, produced tremendous psychological upheaval for the technologically simple peoples of the interior. In both cases, a variety of movements arose in which charismatic visionaries offered both a diagnosis as to why these things had happened and a formula for changing society to accommodate the dislocations. The Seneca prophet Handsome Lake, for example, urged his people to adopt Western agricultural practices, to stop selling land to whites, to give up alcohol, and to seek formal education.

· · · · ·

ELY S. PARKER, SENECA CHIEF, ENGINEER, AND UNION GENERAL (1828–1905)

Ely S. Parker, also known as Hasandoanda, "the Reader," epitomized Handsome Lake's prophetic message that the Iroquois should make peace with change. Parker was a descendant of Handsome Lake, and was sent as a boy to learn English at a Baptist Mission school. He continued his studies, first in law and later engineering. Although he passed the bar exam he was denied a license on the pretext that Indians were not citizens of the United States. He nonetheless used his knowledge to defend Seneca land claims in Washington and collaborated with Lewis H. Morgan on the latter's League of the Iroquois (1851), a classic of anthropological research that did much to establish ethnology as a scientific discipline in the United States. His efforts at defending Seneca interests led to his being named the Wolf clan's Donehogawa, "Keeper of the Western Door," one of the major titles of the Iroquois Confederacy. When the Civil War broke out he enlisted as an officer of engineers and later became Ulysses S. Grant's military secretary. It was Parker who transcribed the articles of surrender for Robert E. Lee's army at Appomattox Court House in 1865 at the end of the Civil War. He left that army in 1867 after rising to the rank of brigadier general. In 1869 Grant appointed him Commissioner of Indian Affairs, a post Parker used to attempt a reform of United States–Indian policy. His criticisms of government corruption, army ineptitude, and racism made him powerful enemies, and a congressional committee accused him of embezzlement. Parker was cleared of all charges but left government service to pursue business interests, making and losing several fortunes in the rough-and-tumble world of nineteenth-century American capitalism.

Ely S. Parker, shown here in an undated photograph, epitomized Seneca prophet Handsome Lake's message that his people should make peace with change.

· · · · ·

Charisma and Routinization

Many of the great world religions appear to have begun as revitalization movements of some sort, as the vision of a charismatic prophet fires the imaginations of people seeking a more comprehensive answer to their problems than they feel is provided by everyday beliefs. Charismatic individuals have emerged at many times and places in the world. It seems that the key to long-term success—and many movements come and go with little long-term effect—has relatively little to do with the prophets, who appear with surprising regularity, but more to do with the development of a group of supporters who are able to institutionalize the movement, sometimes even marginalizing or removing the prophet from a position of actual authority. Max Weber called this "routinization." A particularly

The key to a religion's long-term success appears to have less to do with prophets and more to do with the process of routinization, where a group of supporters institutionalizes the movement. A good example of this is the Mormon Church, over which Brigham Young assumed leadership shortly after the death of the church's founder, Joseph Smith. Young is shown here in a photograph taken between 1855 and 1865.

good example of this is the Church of Jesus Christ of Latter-day Saints, popularly known as the Mormon Church. The original prophet, Joseph Smith, who in 1827 had revealed to him a new Gospel which he and his followers set down as the Book of Mormon, was murdered by an anti-Mormon mob while he was under arrest in a county jail. Soon afterward, Brigham Young assumed leadership, and, among other things, moved most of the followers of the church to an isolated region in the American West, created an effective church bureaucracy and system of finance, and made the leader of the church the authoritative arbiter of revelation, which had not been true in the time of Joseph Smith. It is due in no small part to Brigham Young's vision that the Mormon Church is today the fastest growing and most successful religious movement in the Americas.

Religious Belief and Economic Behavior

The other major contribution Max Weber made to the study of religion was his exploration of the relationship between religious belief systems and economic behavior. Many readers may be familiar with Weber's characterization of the role played by the Protestant Reformation in the rise of European capitalism. Here Weber tried to show that emerging Calvinist beliefs about predestination and material success in the world were intricately bound up in the rise of capitalism in northern Europe. Weber was careful not to say that the Reformation caused capitalism or vice versa. But he did show that ideology and beliefs were not simply a side effect of economic processes, as Marx suggested.

In an interesting parallel exercise, Clifford Geertz looked at economic behavior and religious belief in central Java. There, he noted, a profound local ethic of "shared poverty" that prompted people to redistribute their wealth among as many relatives and neighbors as possible and made the accumulation of capital all but impossible changed when the advent of the steamship made travel to Mecca feasible for ordinary Javanese Muslims. With the possibility of fulfilling an important religious obligation—making a once-in-a-lifetime pilgrimage to Mecca—people had a good reason and a plausible excuse to accumulate rather than share their profits. Having made the pilgrimage, returning *hajis* (as they are called) found that their neighbors regarded them as religious experts. Some would open religious schools, using their students to help in working their lands, a resource that enabled them to acquire more land and greater capital. As with Weber's description of European capitalism, there is no suggestion here that either the steamship or the pilgrimage to Mecca *caused* a kind of Javanese agricultural capitalism,

In an exercise examining the link between religious beliefs and economic behavior, American anthropologist Clifford Geertz found that the advent of steamship travel, which made pilgrimage to Mecca possible for Javanese Muslims, changed the local ethic of shared poverty into one in which people accumulated rather than shared their profits. This photograph taken at the height of the steamship era shows Javanese preparing plumbago for shipping.

but there is simply an observation that two spheres of human endeavor such as religion and economy are intricately linked.

The expansion and apparent success of missionizing religions such as Islam may leave the impression that localized systems of belief are being replaced by more aggressive world religions. Most of the Mixtec of Santiago Nuyoo would today identify themselves as Catholics and look to their parish priest for guidance in spiritual matters. Yet despite having been missionized for hundreds of years by Catholic Church personnel, the Mixtec display a surprising range of unorthodox understandings of Catholicism. Jesus Christ, for example, whom Catholic priests described as "the light of the world," has been identified by the Mixtec and other Mesoamerican people with the Sun. The Sun is an ancient Mesoamerican deity who sacrificed himself so that light and heat might extend over the world; the Sun continues to suffer a daily death as it sets at night, to be reborn in the morning. The Mixtec in effect mapped the Passion of Christ onto their ideas about the Sun, allowing greater resonance for both. Thus they locate Bethlehem, where Christ was born, in the east, while they locate Jerusalem, where Christ died, in the west, where the Sun sets. This kind of rethinking of one faith in terms of another can grow to the point where distinct belief systems emerge. Such faiths were once labeled *syncretistic* by anthropologists, who now avoid the term since all faiths, even the most orthodox forms of the world religions, are historical mixtures of diverse beliefs and practices. In any event, this continuing reinterpretation of the beliefs and practices of world religions in local terms operates in such a way that it is doubtful that any world religion could ever achieve as high a level of orthodoxy among its members as it might wish. Coupled with missionizing strategies that actively seek to create connections with local beliefs, it can result in a situation where the people of a particular religion share a faith in name only.

EIGHT

Ñañuu María Gets Hit by Lightning: People and Their Selves

•

WHILE ON A VISIT TO NUYOO IN 1994 John visited Ñañuu María López, who had provided him with meals when he had first visited Nuyoo a decade earlier. By this time she was quite old and John asked her how she was doing. She replied that she had been sick for several months owing to a terrible burn she had received. Thinking her house had caught fire John immediately asked after the other members of her family, who, she said, were fine; what had happened was she had been hit by lightning while out in the fields. Later on John commented on this chance event and María's miraculous survival to her neighbors, who professed to know nothing about her being hit by lightning. One young man, however, who knew

These figures are from the Codex Bodley, an illuminated Mixtec screenfold book painted just before the Spanish conquest of the region in 1521. It probably left Mexico sometime in the sixteenth century and is now part of the collections of the Bodleian Library in Oxford, England. Some Mixtec writers used umbilical cords in their work to indicate lines of descent. This scene shows Lady One Monkey, an important royal personage around 1300 CE, linked by an umbilical cord to her son Lord Eleven Serpent (he is wearing a mask).

something about the incident, jumped in and said he knew that she had been asleep in her house when the lightning struck; it was her "animal" (*kiti nuvi*) which had been hit by the bolt.

The Mixtec, like other Mesoamerican people, believe that living things that come into the world at the same time are fundamentally linked to one another. An animal and a human born at the same moment will thus share life experiences, are often said to have a single soul, and will, at times, share a consciousness. This latter most often occurs through dreams, which may be interpreted as the world seen through the eyes of one's "coessential" animals (so labeled because the animals and their human counterparts are essentially linked). In Ñañuu María's case her *kiti nuvi* is a small, playful, furry creature called a coati (this had been determined years beforehand through divination and because like the coati she had a special liking for bananas). It was on one of its nocturnal journeys that the coati had been hit by lightning.

The idea of the coessential animal is something that to us seems a bit far-fetched. But the Mixtec case is far from unique, and ethnographers report many examples of traditions that hold that things not physically attached to the body are an intimate part of the self. For the Mixtec the concept of the coessential animal is at least as complex and comprehensive as the id or superego and has no less basis in empirical science: it explains good and bad luck, sudden and even deadly illnesses, the nature of dreams, and even why some individuals have more wealth and power than others, since those with big, ferocious animals such as jaguars stand higher in the social hierarchy than those with small, innocuous animals such as rabbits.

Mixtec thus clearly conceive their selves—their essential being in the world—as not being bounded by the body. María is linked to her *kiti nuvi* not as one discrete whole is linked to another, as one of us feels linked to a lover or a child, but as a fellow creature whose experiences are hers and who shares her experiences in its own dreams, both in a physical as well as a psychic way. In contrast, we in the West tend to view ourselves—and our selves—as consisting at the core of an essentially unitary whole, unique and enduring. Generally, this shows that even so fundamental a facet of our experience of life as our concepts of who and what we are, concepts that seem to constitute a primary basis for common sense, are in fact subject to extraordinary variation from culture to culture. This, in turn has profound consequences for the ways in which societies are constituted socially, economically, and morally. When we in the West see ourselves as persons we tend to see ourselves as *autonomous* individuals, each of us master of our own destiny and not part of a wider continuum of entities that might include a coati. Coming out of that kind of conception of ourselves—and our selves—is a sense of limitless possibility. Children in the United States, for example, are often told in elementary school that "anyone can grow up to be president." Historical and political reality to one side, this notion points to a concept of personhood—and here we use the term *person* to refer to the way ideas about the self articulate a more comprehensive political ideology—which bases personhood on shared capacities and rights. In other words, persons in this context are defined based not on what makes us different, but on what makes us the same. This view of persons is enshrined in the United States Constitution, which endows all citizens with the same social and political rights. In fact the most recent amendments to the constitution have all been concerned with denying the relevance of class, ethnic, racial, religious, or gender differences in social arrangements, economic decision making, and political participation.

There are societies, however, whose ideology of the person appears almost diametrically opposite to the one found in today's United

States Constitution. The Maya, another Mesoamerican people, have a word, *vinik*, that, while originally translated as "individual" by early Spanish observers, turned out on closer inspection to have a different and more subtle set of references. In 1699 a Spanish priest and linguist, Father Francisco Varea, pointed out that the word *vinik* "does not mean person . . . there is no word in this language to say "my person" or "your person" . . . (it means rather) people of my nation. . . ." Father Varea, who was interested in communicating Spanish conceptions of personal responsibility for one's salvation, proposed instead to introduce the Spanish word "*persona*" in translations of scripture, since the idea, for example, of "three persons in one God" would come out, if *vinik* were used, as "three peoples in one god." *Vinik* in Maya also means "twenty." There are twenty named days in the Mesoamerican calendar, each of which defines a particular destiny. Destiny, for Mesoamerican peoples, encompasses personality, vocation, fortune, and physical attributes, so according to this ideology there were twenty basic types of human being. These types complement and support one another, so that on one day painters are born, on another warriors, on another midwives, and all twenty equal a complete human group— a *vinik*. What the Maya concept of *vinik* points to then is what we call a relational concept of the person. In other words, personhood is not a status that adheres to an individual human being but is something that is the property of collectivities.

Furthermore, if we extend our examples to include the Dou Donggo and other Indonesian peoples, we can see instances in which the concept of personhood is expanded to include beings and even objects that are not human. Dou Donggo, for instance, regard their staple food crop, rice, as a sentient person. Rice has both an everyday name and a secret name, by

Each of the twenty days of the Mesoamerican calendar defined a particular destiny, which encompassed personality, vocation, fortune, and physical attributes. This detail from the iconic Mesoamerican calendar, the Aztec sun stone, is on display at the National Museum of Anthropology in Mexico City.

which it can be conjured. The evening before harvesting the rice grown in swiddens, the members of a Dou Donggo family will go out to the center of their fields and take the rice an offering of food, betel, and rice wine, and inform the rice that they intend to harvest the next day, explaining that they do this for their own health and sustenance. The next day the unmarried women of the family don their finest clothes to show honor to the rice they are about to harvest by cutting off the stalks an arm's length below the panicle. Their small finger-knives are held concealed in their hands so as not to unduly alarm the rice. The harvested rice is gathered into great shocks and later transported to granaries in the village. There it is stored until needed, when the women remove a little at a time and pound the

Harvesting rice in Donggo. A young woman pauses while harvesting swidden rice in Donggo. To honor the rice, which Dou Donggo think of as a sentient being, she is wearing her finest clothes. Note the delicate "finger knife" in her right hand, which conceals the blade so as not to unduly distress the rice. Dou Donggo feel very differently about more recently introduced high-yield strains, which are harvested by men using sickles.

grains free of the husks in wooden mortars. Rice kept this way and brought out to feed guests is said to replenish itself magically in the granary. All in all, the Dou Donggo endeavor to treat the grain they depend on with respect and affection and very much as they would a fellow human.

In more recent years Dou Donngo farmers have had to shift in part to growing a variety of high-yield "miracle" rice in irrigated and rain-fed paddy fields. This rice is harvested with little ceremony by men using sickles and is processed immediately by holding the sheaves against a rotating drum studded with long spikes that knock the grains from the husks to be stuffed into burlap sacks. This rice is most often grown for sale rather than home consumption, but many men nevertheless feel uncomfortable treating rice in so violent and brutal a fashion. It is certainly not rice anyone would choose to serve a guest, much less rice that one would expect could discern hospitable intentions and replenish itself. The extension of a kind of personhood to the commodity upon which the Dou Donggo so completely depend (rice is eaten at every meal) provides them with a means of fleshing out a technical economic activity into a richer and more satisfying emotional and, one might say, spiritual exercise.

By way of contrast, we may return to Mesoamerica in the sixteenth century. Historical sources tell us that some children were not endowed with personhood; they were said to be "useless," were unnamed, and were shunned by others. The twenty days of the Mesoamerican calendar divide the solar year into eighteen months, with five unnamed or unlucky days at the end of the year. These days were (and in many places today still are) considered to be a kind of time out of time and were marked by the strict observance of taboos, fasting, and ritual since it was feared any number of bad things might occur, not least of which was the end of the world. Those unfortunates born during this time would not have a destiny—in other words, they would lack the most fundamental aspects of identity. Some ethnographic and historical sources go as far as to describe the children born during the five nameless

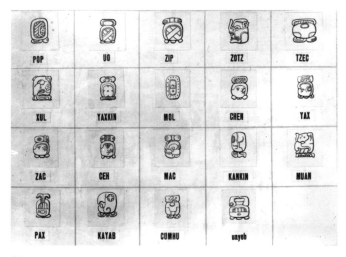

Not all human beings were considered persons in sixteenth-century Mesoamerica. Children who were born on one of the five unlucky days at the end of the year were said to be useless, were unnamed, and were shunned. These Mayan pictograms represent the eighteen months of the solar year, as well as the *uayeb*, the group of five unnamed or unlucky days.

days as lacking a definite physical form, and if they sickened they were not treated, but left to die. In Mesoamerica then, not all human beings were automatically considered persons, that is, endowed with the same basic rights and obligations as everyone else. Consistent with the relational concept of personhood we discussed earlier, these unfortunates were thus left without a place in the group, and forced out of society altogether.

The Self in Sickness and in Health

Concepts of person and self, then, are what anthropologists call culturally constructed. By this we mean that ideas about the world and the people in it that seem quite obvious and ordinary to the members of a culture are in fact the products of a specific historical tradition and differ from one culture to another. Culturally constructed concepts are also reinforced in the individual through their frequent—even constant—use in daily life. At the same time these concepts function within social and political regimes, so that they naturalize things like hierarchy and even exploitation.

Medical anthropologists have applied this perspective in coming to grips with the way in which concepts of the body, its parts and its functions, may produce "culture-bound syndromes." It would seem that since the human body is essentially the same everywhere, everyone should get sick in the same way. But they don't. In Latin America there is a widespread syndrome called *susto*, where a frightening or shocking event causes the soul to leave the body, causing depression and a wasting sickness. Indonesians recognize something similar in the experience called *kaget*, where a sudden shock or surprise leads to a momentary lowering of psychic shields, allowing illness to enter. Medical anthropologists dealing with syndromes such as these have found it useful to distinguish between "disease"—sickness caused by a physiological malfunction or agent—and "illness"—sickness brought on by a patient's perception of his or her bodily state. There are sicknesses which are entirely disease, there are sicknesses which are entirely a matter of perception (often called psychosomatic), but most sicknesses represent a combination of the two. Thus *susto* may be something experienced by individuals who are already malnourished or suffering from some kind of infection. But the key point here is that one's perception of one's body and environment has a great deal to do with one's state of relative health or illness. Anorexia and bulimia qualify as culture-bound syndromes which, as many researchers have shown, are tied to an unrealistic perception of bodily beauty. These eating disorders are also sensitive to gender, age, and class: they are found predominantly among white middle-class young women—another indication of the complex interplay between physiology and society. Because these perceptions are often shared by many people, culture-bound syndromes sometimes erupt in epidemics, affecting thousands of people at one time. Medical researchers are becoming increasingly aware of the extraordinary role stress plays in health and illness; surely what a person considers stressful is largely determined by social convention and culturally constructed perceptions. And perceptions do not always have to function in a negative way. Medical researchers have long been well aware of the effectiveness of simple placebos.

· · · · ·

A DOZEN CULTURE-BOUND SYNDROMES

Amok: intense brooding followed by aggressive behavior directed at people and objects. The original cases reported come from Malaysia, but similar behaviors can be found in other parts of Southeast Asia as well as Polynesia, Melanesia, Puerto Rio (where it is called mal de pelea), and among the Navaho.

Bilis (also called colera and munia): in Latin America, a strongly experienced anger or rage that exacerbates existing symptoms by disturbing the core body balance between hot and cold necessary for a healthy life. Chronic fatigue, nervous tension, stomach disturbances, and headaches may result from an attack of bilis.

Brain fag: found in West Africa among high school and university students overwhelmed by class work. Sufferers may have trouble concentrating, remembering, and thinking, and may feel pain, pressure, or tightness around the head and neck and a blurring of vision. John and Peter have found a similar syndrome among undergraduate students in the United States.

Evil eye: although once found throughout Europe, now strongly associated with Mediterranean societies. It is the notion that envy or strong feelings of desire can adversely affect other people, especially children, or damage material possessions. Symptoms include fitful sleep, diarrhea, and vomiting.

Ghost sickness: in Native American societies, bad dreams, weakness, loss of appetite, fainting, fear, and depression suffered as a result of close contact with a corpse.

Hwa-byung: "anger-syndrome" in Korea: insomnia, fatigue, panic, fear of death, indigestion, generalized pain caused by the suppression of anger.

Koro: the fear among South and East Asian populations that a man's penis will recede into his body or a woman's vulva or nipples will recede into her body. In both cases people believe it can lead to death.

· · · · ·

Gender

Surely there is no aspect of the self that is universally more important in determining how we see ourselves and are seen by others, or is more important in determining how we treat others or are treated by them, than gender. In a very real sense this would seem to be an evolutionary inevitability. After all, for a species to be successful, it has to reproduce itself. Since humans reproduce sexually, it only stands to reason that the distinction between male and female is fundamental and ineluctable. Moreover, it is hard to deny that the most important function society performs is the regulation of sex.

Notwithstanding this universal imperative, anthropologists have come to realize the content of the categories of male and female is by no means the same everywhere. A particularly good example is the Sambia of Highland New Guinea. Traditionally boys were trained from an early age to be valiant warriors, since the Sambia were under constant threat of attack from hostile neighbors. The Sambia felt that to become effective male warriors boys needed to undergo a complex series of initiations, part of which was designed to induce the physiological changes necessary for boys to become adult men. As the Sambia saw it, boys lacked a crucial substance necessary to develop muscle, stature, bravery, and the other things characteristic of a successful warrior. This substance, *jurungdu*, was concentrated in semen, which the boys would ingest in the course of homosexual acts during several stages of initiation. As a boy progressed in his initiation he would

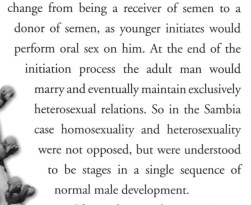

Ideas about what constitutes a proper male or female are not as transparent as they would at first appear, and the role gender plays in culture and society is complex. This male-female duality figurine is from the Remojadas culture on Mexico's Veracruz Gulf Coast.

change from being a receiver of semen to a donor of semen, as younger initiates would perform oral sex on him. At the end of the initiation process the adult man would marry and eventually maintain exclusively heterosexual relations. So in the Sambia case homosexuality and heterosexuality were not opposed, but were understood to be stages in a single sequence of normal male development.

Ideas about what constitutes a "proper" male or female are not as transparent, then, as we might at first assume. Also problematic are assumptions that gender can always be understood in terms of a bipolar and unchanging division of males and females. Like everyone else, the Dou Donggo recognize most people as being either male, *mone*, or female, *siwe*. Some individuals, however, who in our society would probably be called transgendered, are regarded as persons who were intended to become one gender but ended up being born in the body of a person of the opposite gender. They are men who are "*sara siwe*," who "missed at becoming female," or women who are "*sara mone*," who "missed at becoming male." Being *sara siwe* or *sara mone* is regarded as neither shameful or perverse; it is simply an aspect of an individual's self, a product of birth like eye color or stature. For such individuals the usual sexual division of labor observed by the Dou

Donggo is ignored: one *sara siwe* in Doro Ntika became a noted weaver, an occupation ordinarily the exclusive domain of women; this person also dressed as a young woman and joined the young women of the village in harvesting rice. In another instance a *sara mone* decided to accompany the men of the village when they went off to do the heavy labor of clearing the fields in which the village would plant their swidden rice that year. The men made no objection, although they seemed to find it amusing that the *sara mone* would want to take on such an arduous task. But at the end of the day, when they were returning to the village all of them stopped at a bathing pool in the river reserved for men. When the *sara mone* began to disrobe to bathe with them, the men drew the line and refused to permit it.

While the Dou Donggo recognize something of the contingency in masculinity and femininity, and can be said to see gender as something that operates independently of one's physical body, there is evidence that some societies recognize individuals who so combine qualities of femaleness and maleness that they constitute a third and entirely distinct gender. But on the whole, as the Dou Donggo case illustrates, no one quite ignores bodies altogether. Anatomy may not be destiny, but neither is it irrelevant.

Like other social scientists, anthropologists have come to recognize just how complex the role played by gender in culture and society really is and how difficult it is to make generalizations that hold up across space and time. To be sure, some patterns do emerge, although hardly any is without exception. We do observe that relations between the sexes vary tremendously in terms of power and prestige. Among the Dou Donggo, for example, male and female principles are regarded not only as complementary, but as essential to each other and requiring cooperation. While men usually take precedence over women as ritual specialists, for example, many of the more important rituals can be performed only by a man assisted by his wife: when Peter lived in Doro Ntika, the Ncuhi, a sort of high priest in the traditional religion, had effectively been defunct for the years since his wife had died. In many societies in Highland New Guinea, in contrast, men and women are seen as complementary but also as antagonistic. As they approach maturity boys will go to live with their fathers in a communal "men's house" where they live apart from their mothers and younger siblings. Such men's houses are also the centers for cults that can only be described as misogynistic, regarding women as a hostile and dangerous source of pollution, intent upon robbing men of their physical and spiritual power— hence the need for separate living quarters. In yet other times and places the sexes have been regarded as complementary, but with a distinct emphasis on the male domination of women in political, economic, legal, and religious terms, that is, what is generally called patriarchy. In patriarchal societies women have been treated as the property of their fathers and husbands, entitled to little more than protection from men outside the immediate family.

But despite the range of variation in gender relations, from the broadly egalitarian to the strictly patriarchal, these variations are not symmetric: while there are many examples of patriarchal societies in which men dominate women, there are no known examples—outside of myth and legend—of genuinely matriarchal societies in which women dominate men. There are many ways to explain this fact, ranging from the physiological—women bear children and men are almost everywhere the warriors—to the symbolic—men are associated with culture, women with nature—but no explanation seems to satisfy everyone. Perhaps the most trenchant criticism of the various explanations is that men and women interact in such a wide variety of social contexts that choosing the ones where men are dominant distorts the picture. In most cases there are many features of our identity in addition to our gender that enter into our interactions. We can broadly characterize English society of the Victorian era as "patriarchal," for example, but male servants took orders from their female betters, and the sovereign of the most powerful nation on Earth was, of course, a woman. In any event, many sectors of the industrialized societies of Europe and the United States have experienced over the last few decades a radical revision of what were once controlling ideas about gender and sexuality, and a reconfiguration of relationships between males and females. While the developing tolerance of alternate ways of defining gendered identities may not be unique, the emerging symmetry between men and women is of a new sort. If elsewhere in time and space the genders can be seen as either symmetrically or asymmetrically complementary, we in the West now seem to be moving to a view of gender as ideally irrelevant, at least in certain spheres of social life, such as employment.

AFTERWORD: SOME THINGS WE'VE LEARNED

•

A few years ago a student came to Peter with a request to do a course of independent study on the subject of female modesty across cultures. They discussed the idea for a while, Peter confessing that the cross-cultural study of female modesty wasn't a subject about which he knew a great deal, but that without actually investigating the literature he could predict with some confidence what it would show:

- that every culture everywhere has some concept that corresponds to our notion of "modesty";
- that within a given culture it will be applied differently to men and women and differently to the powerful and the less powerful;
- that a given culture will regard its standards of modesty as "natural" rather than culturally determined;
- that "modesty" will have a moral value and a given culture will regard others with stricter standards as prudes and those with looser standards as immoral;
- and that its content will vary widely and arbitrarily across time and space; indeed, that what will be regarded as thoroughly immodest in one place will be regarded as quite proper elsewhere.

This tells us something about the way anthropologists have come to understand the social world. Reduced to its simplest terms, what Peter was able to predict about "female modesty" could be summed up as "People are everywhere the same except in the ways they differ," which is not, admittedly, a very profound statement. Yet in an important sense it *is* what a century of anthropology has taught us, and on closer inspection this is no small thing. It teaches us, for one thing, to take nothing about human beings for granted. When someone begins a peroration with the phrase "but of course, it's human nature to . . . ," start looking for the exit! Because what you are about to hear will most likely reflect the speaker's most deeply held prejudices rather than the product of a genuine cross-cultural understanding. Every time anthropologists have attempted to generate universal rules governing human behavior, the rules have either been proven empirically wrong or are so trivial as to be uninteresting. This is *not* to say that some attempts at figuring out what really is universal to human beings haven't been better than others or that we haven't learned a good deal from such attempts. But it is to say that trying to discern patterns in human social life that are broad enough to include all the variations human cultures have produced, while remaining true to the specific cultural contexts that produce those variations, is a hazardous—if not impossible— undertaking. By the same token, perorations beginning with the phrase "but of course, unlike the West, indigenous people do not . . ." (and here you can fill in the blank with any number of things, such as "mistreat the environment," "suffer from agoraphobia," or "keep slaves"), are equally uninformed by cross-cultural understanding, since they assume an exceptionalism for the West that more often than not turns out to be plain wrong.

Of course we anthropologists have our own epistemological problems as well. No one comes to fieldwork as a tabula rasa. From the beginning of the discipline people have been drawn to anthropology as much by powerful philosophical movements (in the past such things as Marxism, Freudian psychology, and structuralism; today feminism, postcolonial theory, and cultural studies) as by the ethnography of particular groups or the conceptual tools developed within the discipline. Most of us, however, discover that anthropology is at its best when focused on the things that people say and do that do not fit with our expectations. At the same time, those who have been attracted to the discipline out of an abiding love for a particular people face the problem of a kind of parochialism in which matters of little comparative consequence loom large. It may seem we are trying to tear down our own discipline, and in recent years anthropology has been beset by a kind of epistemological crisis, but an honest uncertainty about what we know and how we know it should not be allowed to obscure the real contributions anthropology has made to human beings' understanding of themselves. At its best, anthropology provides the limiting case for people who want to enshrine their own prejudices as universal principles. It has accumulated a record of human inventiveness, resilience, passion, and, alas, depravity, for future generations to contemplate, and it has elaborated unique and valuable tools for understanding the diversity of human cultures and societies. All things considered, that's no mean feat.

FURTHER READING

•

Chapter 1

There are a number of excellent firsthand accounts of ethnographic research. Laura Bohannan's *Return to Laughter* (Doubleday, 1964) was originally published as a novel under the pseudonym Elanore Smith Bowen and it remains a classic of the genre. Nigel Barley's *Adventures in a Mud Hut* (Vanguard, 1983), Paul Rabinow's *Reflections on Fieldwork in Morocco* (University of California Press, 1977), and Jean-Paul Dumont's *The Headman and I* (University of Texas Press, 1978) are all entertaining autobiographical accounts. For a more serious, contemplative description, nothing beats Claude Lévi-Strauss' *Tristes Tropiques* (Athenaeum, 1955; in English translation 1961). There are a number of contemporary critical biographies and critiques of fieldwork methodology. Clifford Geertz provides us with both an autobiographical memoir, *After the Fact: Two Countries, Four Decades, One Anthropologist* (Harvard University Press, 1995), and a consideration of the careers of Lévi-Strauss, Ruth Benedict, and others in *Works and Lives: The Anthropologist as Author* (Stanford University Press, 1985). James Clifford assembled an important set of articles about ethnographic writing in *Writing Culture: The Poetics and Politics of Ethnography* (University of California Press, 1986). George Marcus and Michael Fischer combined to provide an influential critique of ethnographic methods and writing in *Anthropology as Cultural Critique* (University of Chicago Press, 1986), while Marcus has recently edited an anthology of critical essays, *Critical Anthropology Now* (School of American Research Press, 1999). First published in French between 1835 and 1840, see Alexis de Tocqueville's *Democracy in America* (J. Vrin, 1990).

Chapter 2

Alfred Kroeber and Clyde Kluckhohn review definitions of culture in their 1952 *Culture: A Critical Review of Concepts and Definitions* (Vantage Books, 1963). The best intellectual history of the Boasian culture concept is George Stocking's *Race, Culture, and Evolution* (The Free Press, 1968). Clifford Geertz lays out his influential hermeneutic conception of culture in a series of essays published in his *Interpretation of Cultures* (Basic Books, 1973). Edward Said, in *Orientalism* (Routledge and Kegan Paul, 1978), argues that the Orient and Orientals have been represented in ways that reflect the continuing dominance of the West. He has made anthropologists reconsider how their representation of non-Western people might also be colored by colonial and postcolonial interests. In a similar vein Johannes Fabian in *Time and the Other* (Columbia University Press, 1983) examines how anthropology goes about creating its object of study. A non-anthropologist who has been influential in anthropological thinking about culture is Michel Foucault, in whose work, for example, as in *Power/Knowledge: Selected Interviews and Other Writings* (Pantheon Books, 1980), meaning becomes almost synonymous with power.

The sources for quotations in this chapter include Émile Durkheim and Marcel Mauss' *Primitive Classification* (1903; University of Chicago Press, 1969); Claude Lévi-Strauss' *Myth and Meaning* (Schocken, 1978); Dan Sperber's *On Anthropological Knowledge* (Cambridge University Press, 1985); and Robert Murphy's *Cultural and Social Anthropology: An Overture* (Prentice-Hall, 1986), which we consider the best short introduction—preceding this one, of course!

Chapter 3

There are a number of good introductions to classic social theory. R. Jon McGee and Richard Warms have compiled an excellent anthology of classic and contemporary works in *Anthropological Theory: An Introductory History* (Mayfield, 2000). Roger Trigg's *Understanding Social Science: A Philosophical Introduction to the Social Sciences* (Blackwell, 1985) provides a good general overview of many of the issues raised in this chapter. Adam Kuper's *Anthropology and Anthropologists: The Modern British School* (Pica Press, 1985) is an excellent account of the development of British social anthropology from Malinowski until the mid-1980s. Nothing can substitute for reading the greats in the original. For Durkheim we recommend *The Division of Labour in Society* (various editions, 1893) and *Suicide* (various editions, 1897). The standard anthology of Max Weber's works is Gerth and Mills' *From Max Weber: Essays in Sociology* (Oxford University Press, 1958). A standard anthology of Marx is found in Robert Tucker's *The Marx-Engels Reader* (Norton, 1978). Of Bronislaw Malinowski's work his ethnographies stand out as most memorable, particularly *Argonauts of the Western Pacific* (Routledge [Harcourt Brace], 1922) and *The Sexual Lives of Savages* (Kegan Paul [Dutton], 1957); readers interested in his more theoretical essays will want to have a look at *A Scientific Theory of Culture, and Other Essays* (Oxford University Press, 1944). The best collection of essays by A. R. Radcliffe-Brown is in *Structure and Function in Primitive Society* (Free Press, 1961). For Erving Goffman on "total institutions," see his book *Asylums* (Aldine, 1962) and also his classic *The Presentation of Self in Everyday Life* (Doubleday, 1959). The work of Pierre Bourdieu on social reproduction, in particular *Distinction: A Social Critique of the Judgement of Taste* (Harvard University Press, 1984), makes fascinating reading.

Chapter 4

Introductory discussions of anthropological work on marriage and kinship can be found in Roger Keesing's *Kin Groups and Social Structure* (Holt, Rinehart and Winston, 1975) and Robin Fox's *Kinship and Marriage: An Anthropological Perspective* (Penguin, 1967). A useful manual for kinship studies is A. J. Bernard and Anthony Good's *Research Practices in the Study of Kinship* (Academic Press, 1984). David Schneider's *A Critique of the Study of Kinship* (University of Michigan Press, 1984) is a brilliant critical analysis of the way kinship has been conceived and studied. *The Woman in the Body: A Cultural Analysis of Reproduction*, by Emily Martin (Beacon Press, 1987), focuses the lens of anthropological work on the cultural construction of sex, pregnancy, childbirth and other physiological processes surrounding reproduction on Western scientific discourses on women's bodies. Beth Conklin, in *Consuming Grief* (University of Texas Press, 2001), shows how fine attention to the way kin are conceived as connected to themselves and the wider environment helps to make sense of an Amazonian practice Westerners have found disturbing: mortuary cannibalism.

Chapter 5

Much of the bibliography cited for Chapter 3 pertains to this chapter as well, particularly the references to Durkheim and Weber. Although the general reader will find some of the essays difficult, Nicholas Dirks, Geoff Eley, and Sherry Ortner have assembled a terrific anthology, *Culture/Power/History* (Princeton University Press, 1994), that brings together a number of important contemporary voices concerning issues raised in this chapter. An important recent contribution to the study of modernity is Anthony Giddens' *Modernity and Self-Identity: Self and Society in the Late Modern Age* (Stanford, 1990). See Claude Lévi-Strauss' *Totemism* (Beacon, 1963) for a fascinating work on that subject. The Norwegian anthropologist Fredrik Barth's *Ethnic Groups and Boundaries* (Little, Brown, 1969) is dated, but remains the best general introduction to the subject of ethnicity. Readers interested in processes of globalization will find Arjun Appadurai's *Modernity at Large: Cultural Dimensions of Globalization* (University of Minnesota Press, 1996) most intriguing, as they will Mike Featherstone's anthology *Global Culture: Nationalism, Globalization and Modernity* (Sage, 1990).

Chapter 6

The classic statement on gift exchange is *The Gift* by Marcel Mauss (Routledge and Kegan Paul, 1990). An attempt to formally model gift exchange is contained in Chris Gregory's *Gifts and Commodities* (Academic Press, 1982). Helen Codere's *Fighting with Property: A Study of Kwakiutl Potlatching and Warfare, 1892–1930* (American Ethnological Society, Monograph 18, 1986) presents a historical account of the Kwakiutl potlatch. In *"The Gift*, The Indian Gift, and 'The Indian Gift'"* (*Man* 21: 453–473, 1986), Jonathan Parry shows how local gift exchange institutions do not necessarily conform to the universal pattern identified by Mauss. In an important essay in *The Social Life of Things* (Arjun Appadurai [ed.], Cambridge University Press, 1986) Igor Kopytoff proposes that we view objects not as "gifts" or "commodities" but as moving through different exchange and value regimes in the course of their biographies. The social and cultural processes that guide demand are the subjects of *The World of Goods* by Mary Douglas and Baron Isherwood (Basic Books, 1979). In *Distinction* (Routledge and Kegan Paul, 1984), Pierre Bourdieu examines the way consumption reflects the identities of social groups and the differences between them. The essays in Jonathan Parry and Maurice Block's *Money and the Morality of Exchange* (Cambridge University Press, 1989) illustrate the various moral and social regimes which money can underwrite, as well as undermine. The often disastrous effects of market involvement on the kinds of people anthropologists traditionally have studied is illustrated in Eric Wolf's *Europe and the People Without History* (University of California Press, 1982); Wolf also cautions against treating cultures as homogeneous or bounded wholes, but sees groups such as Kachin opium growers, Caribbean sugarcane cutters, and English shop floor workers as parts of a single worldwide division of labor.

Chapter 7

There is an abundance of work done in the anthropology of religion. For the theoretical and ethnographic instances given in this chapter we refer you to Émile Durkheim's *Elementary Forms of the Religious Life* (various editions, 1912) and Max Weber's *Protestant Ethic and the Spirit of Capitalism* (Scribners, 1958) as well as the Gerth and Mills anthology mentioned above. Anthony F. C. Wallace's *The Death and Rebirth of the*

Seneca (Knopf, 1970) tells the story of one "revitalization movement." The ethnographic and theoretical works of Victor W. Turner on life-crisis and other ritual, notably *The Forest of Symbols* (Cornell University Press, 1982) and *Dramas, Fields, and Metaphors* (1985), have been widely influential both in and out of anthropology.

Chapter 8

An excellent discussion of the concept of the person in anthropology and other fields is in M. S. Carrithers, S. Cohen, and S. Lukes (eds.), *The Category of the Person* (Oxford University Press, 1985). For overviews of medical anthropology and the cultural meaning of illness see Arthur Kleinman's *Patients and Healers in the Context of Culture* (University of California Press, 1980) and Mark Nichter's edited collection *Anthropological Approaches to the Study of Ethnomedicine* (Gordon and Breach, 1992). The Sambia are described by Gilbert Herdt in his *The Guardians of the Flutes* (McGraw Hill, 1981). Research challenging the idea that sex and gender are universally dichotomous categories can be found in *Third Sex, Third Gender: Beyond Sexual Dimorphism in Culture and History* (G. Herdt [ed.], Zone Books, 1994). A focus on the complexities in the relationships between men and women and their counterbalancing powers can be found in the collection of essays edited by Peggy Sanday and Ruth Goodenough *Beyond the Second Sex: New Directions in the Anthropology of Gender* (University of Pennsylvania Press, 1990).

INDEX

•

Note: Page numbers in *italics* include illustrations and photographs/captions.

language of, 6
living in Donggo, 6–8
marriage/family of, 22, 24, 104–7,
    110, 115–16
naming traditions of, 131–32
personhood and, 182
religion of, 4–8, 120–24, 130–32,
    141, 164–67, 192
seasons, 165–66
spirits and, 164–67, 182–84
Douglas, Mary, 107, 108
Dou Mbojo, 4
dowry, 107
Durkheim, Émile, 61, 77
    classification systems and, 56
    coherence of society and, 124–25
    collective consciousness of, 99
    collective effervescence and, 127
    collective representation and, 127–28,
        141
    Division of Labour in Society by,
        124–26
    influencing Radcliffe-Brown, 84
    mechanical/organic solidarity and, 90,
        95, 126, 127
    religion and, 167
    Suicide by, 99–100

economy
    of Bolivia, 29
    capitalism and, 175, 176
    cash, 163
    of Doro Ntika, 8
    of Dou Donggo, 162–63
    market exchanges in, 160–63
    organizations for, 144
    power relations and, 155–56

production and, 156
reciprocal exchange and, 150–53
religion and, 175–77, 176
shared descent and, 118
society and, 87
subsistence, 162
elders
    ama Balo as, 23, 164–65
    ama Tife as, 19, 20
    exacting justice, 19–23, 20, 98–99
    governing, 93
    making offerings, 164, 165
Elementary Structures of Kinship (Lévi-
        Strauss), 86
embodiment theory, 68
enchantment theory, 92, 95
environment, 50, 51, 69
ethics, 33, 42–45
ethnicity, 30, 129–33, 135–36
ethnocentrism, 69
ethnography, 3
    definition of, 17
    ethics of, 42–45
    ethnographic present and, 33, 34–35
    fieldwork. See fieldwork
    methodology of, 17–18, 22–24
    observation and. See participant
        observation
    oral histories and, 21
    outsider's perspective in, 40–42
    salvage, 38–39
    specialized fields in, 26
    techniques in, 32
    types of, 29–31
ethnoscience, 57
Evans-Pritchard, E. E., 79
    levirate marriage and, 109–10

PICTURE CREDITS

•

COURTESY OF PETER JUST: viii, 20, 23, 107, 130, 132, 152, 160, 164, 184

MARY EVANS PICTURE LIBRARY: 78, 82–83

COURTESY OF JOHN POHL: ii

COURTESY OF PRINTS & PHOTOGRAPHS DIVISION, LIBRARY OF CONGRESS: 2r: LC-USZ62-36677; 30: LC-DIG-ggbain-30460; 31: LC-USZ62-100043; 41: LC-USZ62-116351; 51: LC-USZ62-112765; 74: LC-DIG-ppmsca-05950; 80: LC-USZ62-134202; 91: LC-USZ62-74580; 119: LC-P87-8011A; 122: LC-USZ62-135989; 124–25: LC-DIG-pga-03090; 134: LC-USZ62-136354; 138: LC-USZC4-4556; 142: LC-DIG-matpc-06806; 148: LC-DIG-det-4a27118; 157: LC-USZ62-116525; 171: LC-USW33-000865-C; 174: LC-DIG-cwpbh-01671; 176: LC-DIG-ggbain-30930

COURTESY OF DAVID STUART: 178

COURTESY OF UNIVERSITY OF TEXAS LIBRARIES: 67

COURTESY OF WIKIMEDIA COMMONS: 6: Brahminic ascetic/Upload by Gryffindor; 10: Codex Vindobonensis; 37: Joseph von Fraunhofer demonstrating the spectroscope, photogravure from a painting by Richard Wimmer; 53: Bees with brood/Upload by Waugsberg; 87: German Karl Marx stamp; 102: Ferdinand Zeppelin family; 106: *The Arranged Marriage*; 108: Marriage certificate of the last Mughal ruler; 118: Ancestor figure/Upload by Jastrow; 129: School of untouchables near Bangalore by Lady Ottoline Morrell; 154: Klallam people at Port Townsend; 168: Baining fire dancer/Upload by Taro Taylor from Sydney, Australia; 173: Ely S. Parker/Original upload by Hlj at en.wikipedia; 183: Aztec sun stone/Upload by Wolfgang Sauber; 190: Male-female duality figure from Remojadas/Upload by Madman2001